Gardening
Mercies

Gardening Mercies

FINDING GOD IN YOUR GARDEN

LAURIE OSTBY KEHLER

BETHANYHOUSE

www.bethanyhouse.com

Published by Bethany House Publishers
A Ministry of Bethany Fellowship International
11400 Hampshire Avenue South
Minneapolis, Minnesota 55438
www.bethanyhouse.com

Printed in the United States of America

Library of Congress Cataloging-in-Publication Data

Kehler, Laurie Ostby.
    Gardening mercies : finding God in your garden / by Laurie Ostby Kehler.
        p.   cm.
    ISBN 0-7642-2393-3 (hardcover)
    1. Gardeners—Prayer-books and devotions—English.   2. Gardens—Religious aspects—Christianity—Meditations.   I. Title.
    BV4596.G36   K44   2001
    242'.68—dc21

                                                                    00-012966

Dedication

For my mother, Helen Ostby

And my sister, H. Signe Ostby

Two great women,

and two great gardeners

Acknowledgments

Thanks to my critique group: Cathy Armstrong, Barbara Milligan, Pat Sikora, and Judy Squier for all your encouragement, editing, and willingness to do "homework." Thanks also to Janet Kobobel Grant for last-minute, down-to-the-wire editing help.

Thank you to Steve Laube for believing in this and catching the vision. Thank you Jeff Braun for your editing mastery. Thank you Alison Curtis for your marketing enthusiasm. Thank you Paul Higdon for making it lovely.

Mountains of thanks to the unnamed people at Bethany House for their sensitivity and commitment to this project.

And finally, thank you Tom for always believing in me and encouraging me.

Laurie Ostby Kehler is the daughter and granddaughter of award-winning gardening mavens. While she originally considered gardening as hot, sweaty, dirty work, she has seen the light and is now a self-confessed gardening fanatic. Laurie and her husband, Tom, live in the San Francisco Bay Area.

For more information regarding speaking engagements and additional materials, you can e-mail her at: Laurie@LKbooks.com.

Or, you can send a self-addressed stamped envelope to:

Laurie Ostby Kehler
P. O. Box 4026
Los Altos, CA 94024-4053

Visit her Web site at: *www.LKbooks.com.*

Table of Contents

Parents usually won't tell you they have a favorite child, or if they do, they'll say something like, "I love William best because of the way he always sees what needs to be done and does it. And I love Emily best because she always loves the underdogs of life. And I love Matthew best because he loves everyone he's ever met and he's a total charmer." They can't commit to having an absolute favorite above all others.

That's exactly how I feel about several of my plants. In the spring, my pink jasmine is my favorite plant. It grows over the fence at the back of the house, right outside our bathroom window. Although the windows above it are narrow, the perfume wafts in and scents the entire house. You can even enjoy the fragrance from the front yard. It's an instant mood lifter. I'm also nuts and nostalgic about my wisteria at this time of year. It drapes its violet panicles with drama and casual sexiness over the house eaves and back fence. Like the jasmine, the wisteria has a knockout fragrance, and it will forever remind me of my visit to the Carolinas in the spring. It has such an elegant, genteel, southern character.

As these two climbers begin to fade, my favorite "impossible dreams" come into their own: my tree peonies. I was so disappointed when I moved out West to discover that herbaceous peonies wouldn't grow here. As a child I had loved their gigantic many-petaled blossoms. My mother would snip some pastel pink ones and float the tissue-paper flowers in an elegant bowl in the dining room. Fortunately, I discovered that my impossible dream for peonies could be realized with *tree* peonies. They grow well here. There aren't as many varieties in this form, but they are big and dramatic, sometimes fragrant, and remind me of home.

In early summer the love of my life comes into bloom—roses. The antique ones, the modern ones, all unfurl their velvet petals and release their musky scents. They have elegant and nostalgic names—Souvenir de la Malmaison, Madame Pierre Oger, Jacques Cartier, Tournament of Roses, Glory Days, Brother Cadfael, to name a few. One of them, Tropicana, reminds me of my grandmother. Despite its intense orange color, the Tropicana was her favorite rose, so I grow it too. Many of the roses commemorate special events, like anniversaries, so a stroll through the rose garden is filled with warm, favorite memories.

Any plant that will give me a great shade of blue is a favorite of mine. I find this in my *Caryopteris* (bluebeard). It's a wonderful shrub, about three feet tall, that has intense dark blue flowers—not at all purplish. My perennial salvias also offer a nice shade of blue that contrasts with the surrounding pink roses.

The lilies are the celebrities of the garden. They are gorgeous and fragrant; unfortunately, they don't bloom for a long season. But when they do, I get out my camera in adoration. The nostalgic favorite is a huge Oriental white lily called Casablanca. My bridesmaids and I carried this lily in my wedding. Whenever I order flowers for someone, I see if the florist can add some of these.

When the miniature Shasta daisies bloom, they always make me smile. Daisies are not special—they are very common—but they are such a happy flower.

The dahlias are my ugly ducklings. At least I used to think of them that way. Now they are my favorite "faithfuls" of the garden. No matter how long the growing season, the dahlias never stop blooming. They are plants I can depend on. I used to think dahlias were too common, their blooms almost garish. But I've come to discover that they have many types of blooms (cactus, semi-cactus, collarette, single, ball, pompon, formal decorative and informal decorative, peony, and water lily). Dahlias come in a staggering variety of colors as well; there's a dahlia for the pickiest of gardeners. Dahlias are my favorite flower for vases. If you want no-fail arrangements for the house that last a long time, grow dahlias.[1]

In the fall I'm filled with wonder, delight, and gratitude as I watch our Golden Delicious apple tree become laden with fruit. It is always such a miracle to see it go from bare branches to masses of blossoms to huge, tantalizing apples every year.

My favorite flower in the winter is one you can barely see: Russian

---

[1] Swan Island Dahlias in Canby, Oregon, is a great source for dahlias (503-266-7711) or *www.dahlias.com.*

olive or *Elaeagnus angustifolia* (doesn't that just roll off your tongue?). This shrub's flowers are about the size of a baby's fingernail, but oh, the fragrance! The first time I encountered them was in my sister's garden. We were strolling through on a wintry evening at twilight. Suddenly I stopped and clutched her arm. "What *is* that incredible fragrance?" It was her Russian olive. I was amazed and enchanted that such a fragrant flower could bloom at that time of year. There's an area a few miles from my house with a dense planting of Russian olives. Whenever I ride my bicycle past, I inhale deeply so as to fill my lungs with their clovelike scent.

We all have our favorites in life, and we all want to *be* someone's favorite. To be told "You are my *favorite* one" is a delicious feeling.

The mother of the sons of Zebedee wanted this favoritism for her sons. In the book of Matthew she boldly went up to Jesus and asked, "Grant that one of these two sons of mine may sit at your right and the other at your left in your kingdom." Two thousand years later we laugh and are astonished at her brazenness and chutzpah. Yet Jesus tactfully answered her, "To sit at my right or left is not for me to grant. These places belong to those for whom they have been prepared by my Father."

The disciples each wanted to be the favorite one as well. The Gospel of Luke records that even during the Last Supper, right after Jesus broke bread and said, "This cup is the new covenant in my blood, which is poured out for you," the disciples immediately began to argue. Luke records, "A dispute arose among them as to which of them was considered to be greatest." That amazes me. In the middle of one of the most significant moments in history, a scene that we revere and act out in churches around the world, the disciples were behaving like children. They each wanted to be the favorite, the special one. Sitting here two thousand years later, we think we would never be so small-minded and selfish. Oh, but we are.

A large Bible study that I am a part of recently asked me to consider becoming a discussion leader for a small group. When I was mulling this over with my husband, he asked me, "What are the reasons you would do it?" I found my answers to be less than flattering to my character.

Was I concerned about how this position would glorify God? No, I was thinking about prestige. *Well, it would be nice to be in the inner circle*, I first thought. I *was* considering how I could best serve God with my talents when they asked me, but I found it interesting that my first thought was self-oriented. When I asked my current small group leader why she liked being in that role, the first reason she came up with (among other, more godly ones) was "It's certainly fun to be in the leaders' group...." I appreciated her honesty; I didn't feel so alone. I *do* want to serve God, I *do* want to be in the middle of His will, but my selfish nature tends to jump in and usurp the greater goal. We all want to feel special, included, and part of the favorite group.

Sometimes things we've done in our past hold us back from feeling as if we are one of God's favorites. We think the do-gooders and those whose pasts are free from sexual sin, stealing, addictions, lying, and murder are in better standing with God. Sure, we may have our salvation, but we feel as if we're squeaking into heaven to sit in the back row while the do-gooders are front and center. But this is incorrect. God doesn't see us that way. He tells us, "My thoughts are not your thoughts, neither are your ways my ways" (Isaiah 55:8). In another passage God says, "The Lord does not look at the things man looks at. Man looks at the outward appearance, but the Lord looks at the heart" (1 Samuel 16:7).

God has told us in His Word that *we* are his favorites. After each of His creative acts in the book of Genesis, Scripture says, "And God saw that it was good." But after the creation of *humankind*, it says, "and it was *very* good." He has bestowed on us tender titles indicating what He thinks of us. Titles like *children of God* (Romans 8:16), *heirs of God and co-heirs with Christ* (Romans 8:17), *sons and daughters of God* (2 Corinthians 6:18), *friends of Christ* (John 15:15), *loved and chosen by God* (1 Thessalonians 1:4), to name just a few. Even more to the point, in Romans 8, we are told that we can call the creator of the universe, God Almighty, *Abba,* which means Daddy (Romans 8:15). Throughout the Bible, God has tried to communicate His tender heart toward us.

One of my favorite stories about knowing and tasting God's favoritism comes from Brennan Manning's book, *Abba's Child.* He relates a story about a priest from Detroit, Edward Farrell, who went on vacation to Ireland. One morning before dawn, Edward and his eighty-year-old uncle Seamus were walking along the shores of Lake Killarney. They stopped to watch the sunrise in silence.

Suddenly the uncle turned and went skipping down the road. He was radiant, beaming, smiling from ear to ear.

His nephew said, "Uncle Seamus, you really look happy."

"I am, lad."

"Want to tell me why?"

His eighty-year-old uncle replied, "Yes, you see, my Abba is very fond of me."[2]

When I stroll about my favorites in the garden at twilight, I'm amazed at the beauty and diversity in God's creative handiwork. I treasure just sitting and being surrounded by it all—the humming bees, the chattering birds. And instead of thinking about how much I'm *not* doing, instead of comparing myself to others or thinking about how little I've prayed lately, I try to remember He's my *Abba*—Father. I'm one of His favorites, and He's very fond of me.

---

[2] Brennan Manning, *Abba's Child* (Colorado Springs: NavPress, 1994).

Growing Points

I. ❧ What are some of your favorite plants?

2. ❧ Who in your life has made you feel as if you were a favorite?

3. ❧ Which of the familiar titles that God bestows on us do you like the best and why?

4. ❧ Have you ever felt like Uncle Seamus? What was the setting or the reason?

A Pleasing Aroma

One of the most thrilling parts of gardening is the fragrance. To sit in your yard or walk up to the front door and have a beautiful, alluring scent, heavy with summer, come wafting by your nose is a little bit of heaven. Okay, maybe a lot of heaven.

Two of my all-time favorite plants for pungent, knock-your-socks-off fragrance are tuberoses and gardenias. These flowers are so strong that a single stem of tuberose or a blossom of gardenia will perfume an entire room. You want more romance? A touch of Hawaii or some exotic location? Wonder what a "heady" experience is? Grow these flowers; the scents are to die for.

Although tuberoses grow well here in California, you can grow them just about anywhere, because they were my grandmother's favorite flower, and she grew them in Wisconsin. They prefer a very warm, sunny location. Just as they start to open, you'll probably need to watch for (and spray for) thrips. After you hit a certain age, you might not even be able to *see* thrips. They were hard for me to spot back in my early thirties. They are minuscule little slivers of bugs that suck the life out of your blossoms. They are particularly attracted to the color white (and gardenias are white too).

Gardenias also like sun, but not as much. And they love acid and iron supplements. They just can't get enough. If you use a supplement once every three or four weeks, you will be rewarded with deep green, robust plants.

I have a soft spot in my heart for gardenias because of all the memories associated with them. They were the corsage of choice for high school dances. My wedding bouquet had them in it. And my mother used to pin them on the pillows of sick people she visited in the hospital so they could enjoy the intense fragrance.

Sweltering summer nights when it's so hot and uncomfortable that you can barely fall asleep are the best for these flowers. The most elegant way to enjoy gardenias is to cut the blossom with little or no stem, leaving just one or two leaves for accent. Then find a bowl (florists use glass ones specifically for this purpose), fill it half full with water, and float a couple blossoms in it. Place it by your bed a few hours before retiring. Voilà! You've just created a romantic getaway.

When you enter your bedroom later that evening, you will be transported by the fragrance.

On warm nights, it wafts around the room like a silken net, making you feel as if you were in a sultry, tropical locale. As you toss and turn in bed, the fragrance lifts and settles about you, caressing you into sweet dreams.

Often, I leave these blossoms in the bowl, or tuberoses in a vase, far beyond their attractive state. They have turned brown and the water is discolored, but I still don't throw them out. This is because I've realized that as these flowers turn brown and unsightly, their aroma becomes even more intense. They exude a deeper sweetness as they die.

Our lives can be that way. As we get closer and closer to the end of our days, the actions and attitudes we exude can be a sweet aroma to those around us. Unlike some elderly people who are bitter and nasty and happy to make everyone around them listen to their endless complaints, there are those whose life purpose is to serve others. They can't talk enough about the blessings they are enjoying. I'm sure they have aches and pains, too, but they don't focus on those things.

My father-in-law, Albert Kehler, is that way. His prayer has always been "Lord, send me to someone who needs me." He has the most positive, sweet nature. He developed this through many years as a country preacher, living by faith for most of his life and not knowing where or when the next meal and paycheck were coming from. Hell could be freezing over, and he would marvel at the excitement that we were all going to have when we went ice skating. He creates a sweet environment just by his attitude. As he advances into his eighties, he just smells better and better.

Sacrifice, to God, is a sweet aroma. After being rescued from the flood, Noah built an altar to the Lord and offered burnt offerings in thanksgiving. Genesis 8:21 in the New International Version says it was a "pleasing aroma." The New American Standard Bible says it this way: "And the Lord smelled the soothing aroma."

When we offer to God the death of our own wills and agendas, it is an aromatic sacrifice to Him. Psalm 51:17 says, "The sacrifices of God are a broken spirit; a broken and contrite heart, O God, you will not despise." And Hebrews 13:15 says, "Through Jesus, therefore, let us continually offer to God a sacrifice of praise—the fruit of lips that confess his name." The disciples made an offering when they left everything to follow Jesus. We do it when we offer up our agendas and plans for our lives, our hopes and dreams, in order to let God do with us as He wants. And because of Jesus' sacrifice of dying on the cross on our behalf, God "always leads us in His triumph in Christ, and manifests *through us* the sweet aroma of the knowledge of Him in every place" (2 Corinthians 2:14 NASB).

Have you had to submit to an unfair situation? Have you had to give up on your script for your life? It may seem like all hope and life are being snuffed out. Your plans are turning brown and decayed. But the sweet smell you exude to Him as you willingly give up your plans for His is a death *and* a beginning. He promises us that.

Be confident that the Master Gardener is in charge and He knows how you feel. He's been there, done that. He was nailed to a cross. It was the end of His earthly friendships and His relationship with His family. But it was also the beginning of the sweet smell of success. As His life was being pressed out of Him while He hung on the cross, an aromatic fragrance began to fill heaven. It was the sweet smell of success, redemption, souls paid for in full.

What an incredible promise: that because of Jesus' work, we have the privilege to be a "soothing aroma" to the creator of the universe and to the hurting world out there. And to Him, it is not death, the end, but a "triumph in Christ."

Now that's a scent to die for.

Growing Points

I. ᴥ Read Genesis 8:15–22. What do these verses tell you about how God feels regarding your gratitude?

2. ᴥ Read 2 Corinthians 2:14–16 and 4:7–12. Can you recall a time when others (either saved or perishing) have noticed a fragrance from you of Christ? Did they like it or dislike it?

3. ᴥ What things can you "die to" in your life that would be a sweet aroma to God?

4. ᴥ What fragrance is God smelling from you now? (Peace? Contentment? Service? Love?)

No Bees

"I want a sort of rough-hewn gazebo, with grapevines running up into it. A little swath of grass by the pool and some perennial plants that I don't have to worry about." My friend was describing to me her plans for her backyard pool area. "Some vines over the fence would be nice, but I told that landscape guy, *'No bees!'*"

"*No bees?*" I said, knowing that you can't have decent fruit or a healthy flower garden without bees. "Why no bees?"

"I don't want little Susie to get stung. Plus, they're a nuisance," she said.

"But how do you expect to have flowers or a garden without bees?" I asked. Secretly I thought she was being ridiculous. Apparently the landscape designer thought so, too, because every time he'd show up to work on the garden he would mutter under his breath about her odd request and punctuate the end of every design discussion with a sarcastic "I know, *no bees!*"

She was adamant. "I don't care how that designer does it— that's his problem—but I don't want any plants that attract bees." If no bees were her goal, I thought cactus plants or a bunch of boulders would be a good choice.

Thinking about that conversation from a few years ago makes me chuckle at the absurdity of it. Today, as I was watering the garden with a hose, bees happily hummed about my lamb's ears plants (*Stachys*), the lavender, and the last few blossoms of the orange tree. As I brushed by the bees, disturbing them from one blossom, they merely moved to another blossom.

I have never been stung in my garden. I suspect that's because most of the bees in my garden are orchard mason bees, *Osmia lignaria*. The mason bee, or blue orchard bee, is native to the United States and is a more efficient pollinator than the honeybee. To pollinate an acre of apples requires 20,000 or more honeybees versus 250 female blue orchard bees. The other nice thing about these bees is that they are solitary. They don't make honey or live in hives, so they have no big nest to defend with a nasty attitude. They are mild-mannered and hardly ever sting people.

Although they don't create and live in hives, these solitary bees do need a home. They prefer holes in wood. Mason bees like the holes to be 1/4 to 3/8 inch in diameter and 3 to 6 inches deep in a pine or fir 4 x 4. You can make a home for them or just order a handy ready-made home from the Territorial Seed Company catalog.[1] This company offers several

---

[1] Territorial Seed Company catalog, 541–942–9547. Web site: *www.territorial-seed.com*.

different bee houses, including a Humble Bumble
Home, a Multi-Species Bee Block, and a Mason
Bee Block, plus several books about bees and how to
raise them.

Any seasoned gardener will tell you that a healthy garden
is one where bees flourish. A garden where pesticides are used
heavily is a dead garden. No bees, no butterflies, and no birds visit a garden that's had its blossoms doused in chemicals.

Bees are a crucial element in pollination. If you want well-formed
and great-tasting fruits and vegetables, bees have to pollinate those blossoms before they can set fruit. Some fruits and vegetables, like pumpkins
and blueberries, won't produce *any* fruit without the assistance of pollinators. Having bees around will give you bigger fruit, better-quality fruit,
and bigger yields.

In California, farmers are starting to panic because there aren't as
many bees these days to pollinate the orchards. (I suspect it's all the
chemicals and pesticides they use.) They are starting to bring in thousands of bees via mail order. My sister and I laugh when we hear this. Our
gardens are full of happy, busy, pollinating bees. We are proud to have
this sign of vitality and health in our gardens. Sure, we might get stung
one day, but it's a risk you have to take if you want a beautiful garden.

My friend wanted a beautiful garden, but no bees.

I understand the desire and need for control in my friend's "No
bees" life. She had suffered under abusive parents and now was having
constant marital trouble herself. She compensated for this by keeping a

meticulous home, and she wanted nature to bend to her will as well.

That's often how I feel about my life. I want a life that is beautiful. Everything under control, going to my plan, my script. If I could control the events around me, I would. (Not that I don't try all the time!) I don't like suffering the stings of life. I want a life like my beautiful flower gardens, but that's not possible without the "bees" of life. Even more importantly, I've noticed that it's the "bees" that make our lives richer and more precious.

When a fruit blossom isn't pollinated properly by our friends the bees, it becomes a stunted, deformed, bad-tasting thing. Have you ever looked at someone's life and seen the same thing? A stunted, deformed life? A life that lacked vitality and purpose?

A very wealthy woman I know of spends her days reading romance novels, watching soap operas, and painting birdhouses. When people comment on how talented she is to paint such nice things, she says, "It helps alleviate the constant boredom of my life." Her biggest struggle in her life is boredom! She lacks vitality and excitement in her life because she is not willing to leave her safe, cozy cocoon. She doesn't want to risk reaching beyond her comfort zone, failing, or being hurt or disappointed, so her life is spent in idle hours while anesthetizing herself with meaningless activities. Her life is sterile. She has no fruit. She isn't touching anybody's life in a meaningful way. She isn't living the abundant life that God meant for her to live.

That's not how life is meant to be. God gave all of us jobs to do (first of all, tend the garden!). In doing the work He gave us, we discover vital

living. If Jesus had to learn obedience and suffering on His path to a fulfilled life, why should you and I be exempt? Would we be able to identify with Him with our problems had He not suffered? So then, how can
this world relate to us if we have not suffered? People are longing for others to be real with them. To unzip their souls, put down the masks, and
say, "I have been disappointed and angry at God. I have been hurt. I have
thought life wasn't fair—but this is how God came through for me." Hard
times pollinate our faith. Hard times give us the opportunity, like pollination, to pass along something to a needy world.

In a flower's life, bees come along and drink nectar. While sunk
deep inside the flower, the bees pick up the flower's pollen on their legs
and abdomen. When the bees visit the next flower for a drink, voilà! That
flower gets some of the pollen from the previous flower. Now the flower
is fertilized, and several weeks later fertile seeds are produced within the
walls of the fruit that was originally a flower. Now that plant is producing
fruit. It is performing as God planned.

One way we can live the fruitful life God designed for us is to "comfort those who are in any affliction with the comfort with which we ourselves are comforted by God" (2 Corinthians 1:4 NASB). Those painful
"bees" in life—the addictions, the disappointments, the heartaches—can
become "pollinators" to your faith. For until you turn around and pass
along what you have learned to another person who needs some comfort,
you won't see or experience the joyful fruit it can produce.

Growing Points

1. ⟡ What painful experiences happened in the apostle Paul's life? (See 2 Corinthians 4:7–10, Acts 14:19–20, Acts 16:22–24)

2. ⟡ Has anybody shared with you how they handled a problem similar to one you have?

3. ⟡ Why do you suppose support groups are so successful and popular in this country?

4. ⟡ What fruit have you seen develop in yourself or others as you've shared your experiences?

Eating dinner at my sister Signe's house is always a thrill. Not just because I love to be with my nephews and niece. Not just because she's a great cook and always tries something new. It's a thrill because part of dinner is often a do-it-yourself affair.

We all hang around the kitchen and chat for a while. Then Signe will ask, "What vegetable do you want to go with your chicken? How about with your salad? Eggplant? Artichokes? Sautéed onions?" You see, at her house, you can pick your lettuce, tomatoes, or whatever vegetable you're hankering for right from her garden beds. It's like those seafood restaurants where you point to your fish or lobster in the tank and say, "I'll take that one, please." Only this is better, because unlike the fish, which may have been flown in and are not in their natural environment, Signe's vegetables have been growing in the healthy soil right outside the door.

I feel as if I'm in Italy, or the south of France, as I saunter out in the late afternoon sun and wander among the raised beds, trying to decide what to eat. The tomatoes, warmed all afternoon by the hot sun, are pungent and beckoning. I pull a few cherry tomatoes off the plants to munch on while I stroll. They explode with a warm sweetness in my mouth, with a taste of all that summer has to offer. Sometimes the eggplants look promising; sometimes the arugula is what tempts me. There is lemon basil, cinnamon basil, and sweet Genovese basil to finger and smell as I consider her living produce stand.[1]

Maybe the biggest thrill I get out of this is knowing how *good* Signe's food is. Good because she grew it herself. Good because she doesn't depend on any chemical pesticides or chemical fertilizer to grow them. Good for me, and fabulous tasting.

I decided to grow my own goodness one year, so I took a carload of my sister's homemade compost, which is mostly horse manure, and planted several heirloom Brandywine tomato plants with it. (You should know that heirloom tomatoes consistently win taste tests, and Brandywine, to me, is the best.) I chose a spot next to the house for additional warmth and dug an extra deep hole. Then I put in lots and lots of the compost and sunk the plant up past several leaf nodes. I found out that more roots are encouraged to grow from these leaf points if you bury them, and more roots mean monster plants. And if you're crazy about tomatoes like I am, you'll do anything short of a rain dance to encourage them.

That year I (or, rather, my Brandywine tomato plant) was the talk

---

[1] The Cook's Garden catalog (800-457-9703 or *www.cooksgarden.com*) is an excellent source for lettuces, tomatoes, and other vegetables.

of the neighborhood. Nobody could believe how huge the plant grew and how many tomatoes it produced. In two consecutive weekends I had fifty or more tomatoes. (I have photos to prove this.) They were huge, big-shouldered pink ones. It was so easy to get a handyman to come over and fix things once he had a taste of my tomatoes. "Oh, I've got *so* many tomatoes again," I'd sigh into the phone. "I don't know what I'm going to do with them!" That got him over here in a hurry because he knew I'd send him home with a shopping bag full of tomatoes for his wife.

Once you've grown your own vegetables, it feels like an abomination to buy them for those high prices at the grocery store. (*Abomination* might sound like a strong word, but when I put an armload of the grocery store's version of "heirloom" tomatoes on the counter and they said, "That'll be ten dollars," it sure felt like an abomination to *me*.) Even though we enjoy and sometimes buy things at local farmers' markets, nothing is as satisfying as growing your own. You know what went into that plant, you know what kind of fertilizer it was fed, and you know that it wasn't tainted by any pollution or chemicals.

I feel the same way about my faith. When I first became a Christian, I depended a lot on other people to feed me. *Their prayers must be more powerful than mine,* I naïvely thought. *God probably seriously listens to them—or at least does their bidding quicker.* I figured if Billy Graham ever prayed for me, I'd have it made—prayers answered. I had never been to a Bible study class or seen a study Bible, so I didn't know that they existed and I didn't know how to study on my own for the answers I sought.

I'll never forget the first Bible study I attended. It was held in the basement of a small Baptist church in Wisconsin. The woman who invited me called it a Sunday school class. I thought I'd had enough Sunday school growing up. I couldn't imagine I'd glean anything from one more parable about the lost sheep. But I was hungry to taste the joy that she was experiencing, so I went. A red-haired man was teaching on Ecclesiastes 12, "Remembering God in Your Youth." It was outstanding. I felt like a woman parched from the desert getting my first drink of pure water. I was riveted to my seat as he explained the poetry of the author. When he talked about "the keepers of the house tremble, and the strong men stoop" representing the hands and legs of an elderly man, I was fascinated. Previously, I had thought the Bible was full of boring, hard to understand stories with little application to my life. Since that day, I've discovered just the opposite is true.

God's Word is a continual feast. There is always something new to learn and savor, even from a passage you thought you understood completely. That's because God himself is limitless. He is omniscient, omnipotent, and omnipresent. You can't outwit Him or come to the end of Him. You'll never get Him all boxed up and neatly shelved. He has no beginning or end. He is an endless well of wisdom, and He invites us to drink and be refreshed. He invites us to a feast: "Taste and see that the Lord is good, blessed is the man who takes refuge in him" (Psalm 34:8). You can

always find some morsel to chew on. In Romans you'll find some meaty doctrine, the Psalms contain the ultimate comfort food, and to me, Galatians, Ephesians, and Philippians are delicious desserts.

Jesus talked about feeding on God's Word. "'My food,' said Jesus, 'is to do the will of him who sent me and to finish his work'" (John 4:34). And, "I am the bread of life. Your forefathers ate manna in the desert, yet they died. But. . . I am the living bread that came down from heaven. If anyone eats of this bread, he will live forever" (John 6:48–51). Clearly, we are encouraged to read and make God's Word our sustenance to grow in our faith. (Isn't it interesting that God in the flesh, Jesus, was placed in a manger—a feeding trough?)

It hurts me to see suffering people taken advantage of. They have shallow roots and haven't taken the time to grow their own faith. They depend on the thoughts, words, and prayers of other Christians who they think have a direct line to God—or a stronger connection than they do. Many people were taken advantage of during the Tammy and Jim Bakker television days. When you're in emotional or physical pain, you'll give just about anything and any amount of money to someone who assures you that they have a direct line to God. (Recently, I heard a great radio interview with Jim Bakker about his new book, *I Was Wrong.* That pretty much tells you where he ended up with his "prosperity gospel" thinking, doesn't it?) So many motivational speakers and preachers can breeze into town and say, "If you just come forward, I KNOW God will answer your prayer!" Well, yes, God will always answer our prayers—maybe not the way we think He should, maybe more than we dreamed He could, but definitely not just because some big name person uttered words for us. So whether you join the throng that's streaming up to the altar or not, your prayers are just as effective. You can talk to God directly. You can grow your own faith.

God himself has asked us to do this. In the book of Jeremiah we read, "Call to me and I will answer you and tell you great and unsearchable things you do not know" (33:3). And Peter, who suffered the anguish of denying Jesus, told us, "Cast all your anxiety on him because he cares for you" (1 Peter 5:7).

The other advantage of growing your own faith is that you become more confident and joyful. You see God answering *your* prayers, *your* questions, revealing himself to *you*. That's a supernatural high! But you can't experience it if you don't put in the time to prepare your soil. Get yourself a good study Bible and find a class or a book to help you do an in-depth study of God's Word. And then, most of all, apply what you learn.

I've seen what a difference it has made in my life. I've gone from an insecure, fearful, angry person to one who confidently handles the Word of God. I can discern error from truth. I know how to test what people (even my pastor) say against the Bible. Do I have it all together? Am I problem-free? Absolutely not. I'm still in that up-and-down growth process of sanctification that Paul talks about in Romans 7. (Behavior that I want to stop, I keep doing. Behavior I'd like to practice, I don't do.) However, I'm getting closer to becoming the mature person described in Jeremiah 17:7–8: "Blessed is the man who trusts in the Lord, whose confidence is in him. He will be like a tree planted by the water that sends out its roots by the stream. It does not fear when heat comes; its leaves are always green. It has no worries in a year of drought and never fails to bear fruit." To enjoy that delicious taste of communion with the creator of the universe, I had to stop depending on other people's faith and instead look into the Bible and grow my own.

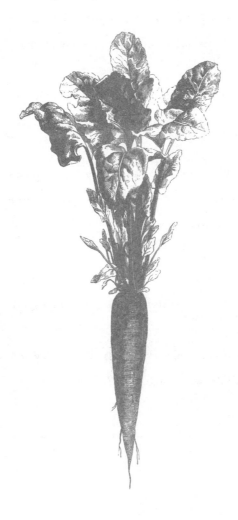

Growing Points

1. ❧ What do Hebrews 5:12 and 2 Timothy 3:16–17 say about the power of God's Word?

2. ❧ Who in your life has fed you knowledge about God or His Word?

3. ❧ When you think about your main spiritual mentors or teachers, what sort of information did they give you? Was it true or false?

4. ❧ Can you apply any of the Bible verses in this chapter to a situation you're going through now?

5. ❧ If you could take a class or study any book of the Bible, what would it be?

✦

To me, the ultimate event planner is not *Martha Stewart Living* magazine. It's a little book of notations I've scribbled in over the years. Because of this diary, or garden journal, I can tell pretty much within a couple of days when certain plants are going to bloom. If it's a year of heavy rain, I know the flowers will be three weeks later. The journal is a great tool for planning. If I want to have a party when the spring bulbs and flowers are in bloom, I just check the journal to find out when that might be. If I want a garden party when the roses are in their full glory, I look in my gardening journal for a history of the first blush of bloom.

This journal also helps me to record and remember what worked before and which plants were abysmal failures. I tend to forget why a certain plant didn't thrive and persuade myself to try it again—unless I look in my garden diary.

A gardening journal or diary can be as detailed or as brief as you like. It's for your reference, not for anyone else's. Below is a sampling of what I record, remember, or fume about in my garden diary.

MARCH 2

Great morning working in the backyard. Did lots of work on back hill, put in perennial primroses. Put in a straggly fern that I dug up from Mary's. Finally put in *Ajuga* that Virginia gave me two years ago! Yanked up gobs of violets—they are spreading everywhere. All the cyclamen are blooming and spreading on hill. The hydrangeas seem to be thriving now that I moved them there. Mole trails *everywhere*. Have put in a "mole pole" that's humming and supposed to get rid of them. Plus using an oil mix.

MARCH 7

Repotted Meyer lemon tree my sister gave me. The orange tree's fruit is fantastic! Put horse manure all over beds by the fountain—can't wait for all that lavender to be hit by the spray this summer. Have *got* to prune the apple tree. The Wayside Gardens[1] trumpet lily bulbs I received were *huge*. Planted this apricot-colored dahlia, Alfred Grille, in pink and white raised bed. I've wanted that particular dahlia of my sister's for so long—I was thrilled when I found it. Divided up Park Princess dahlia for neighbors and potted them.

---

[1] Wayside Gardens catalog, 800-845-1124. Web site: *www.waysidegardens.com.*

APRIL 4

It's been a gorgeous spring. No incessant torrential rains like last year. The pink jasmine is covered in blossoms; I can hardly see any green leaves. When we open the front door, you can smell its seductive scent wafting in through the windows and throughout the house. The wisteria is putting on an elegant show too. It's trying to engulf the back fence and is very happy with the new sturdy wire support that I put up under the roof eaves in the front. When I pass underneath its pungent panicles, I can almost hear Blanche DuBois saying in her southern accent, "I've always depended on the kindness of strangers."

So glad I moved some of the roses around. That Sheer Bliss was trying to *take over* the raised bed. So aggressive. She's doing much better back against the fence. I'll make her duke it out for space with the matilija poppy. May the best lady win.

MAY 5

French Lace roses at end of walkway are in full glory. The blue ground cover morning glories set them off perfectly. Flower Carpet and Ballerina roses are covered in buds. Geraniums by front door are unstoppable—such performers. Started beans, squash, peas in seed flats; they are coming up *great*. Miss my delphiniums. Don't think any are coming back after tree planting and digging around them. The mole solution has killed some of my favorite roses—King's Ransom and the Fairy Tree rose. That's about $70 worth. The company won't replace my plants and don't believe their crummy product is to blame.

MAY 7

Had the trapper out and he caught two of those annoying moles! My neighbors tell me that they have them too. Hope they don't cross streets. Transplanted the tuberoses a few weeks ago to the front area; they are doing great. Cut gobs of roses; every room in house has a bouquet.

JUNE 21

My neighbors think I'm quite the rosarian. This cracks me up. All I did was check the diary for the last time I gave the roses some Epsom salts. It had been too long. It's obvious they are grateful—new shoots all over the place. It seems weird to me that any kind of salt would be good for them, but they do respond well to half a cup every two months.

There's nothing like the sound of a happy little wren singing its heart out just outside your window. Made my day...

AUGUST 12

The tomatoes are starting to come in. Although I

noticed, from looking at my notes in here last summer, I'm not getting as many per plant as I did last year. I wonder why. Maybe it's because I put that one tomato plant by the house last year. I know they crave heat; maybe that's what did it. First picking off Brandywine plant was twenty-five last Saturday. According to what I wrote here last year, I got twice that amount then. Think I'll go back to planting them against the house....

Thanks to my diary, I can remember my mistakes and avoid them in the future. Thanks to my diary, I can recall what worked in the past and apply the same strategy.

Christopher Lloyd and Beth Chatto have written a book, *Dear Friend & Gardener,* that records their gardening triumphs and failures in letters to each other. I found this delightful read when I was in London with my husband.[2] The whole book is simply letters that they've written to one another about what's going on in their gardens. It was like poking my nose into their private garden diaries. I found it fascinating.

On the same trip to London, I poked my nose into Gertrude Jekyll's private garden diary. Gertrude lived in England, where she was and still is revered, even after her death. Gertrude is to gardening what Elvis is to the South. She lived during the Edwardian period and was

---

[2] Beth Chatto and Christopher Lloyd, *Dear Friend & Gardener* (London: Frances Lincoln Ltd., 1998).

famous for her keen eye and sensitive use of color. She was vertically challenged at four feet ten inches tall and very round. One of my favorite garden writers, Cassandra Danz, described Gertrude:

> She could have rolled around her garden if she didn't
> want to walk and she lived to be eighty-nine years old. Since
> longevity seems to be one of the happy by-products of gar-
> dening, if you're just starting out, you have plenty of time to
> develop. She was also legally blind for the last forty years of
> her life. She wore thick Coke-bottle glasses that didn't do her
> much good. They didn't do her appearance much good,
> either....
>
> She had pink roses cascading over walls, garlands of
> clematis draped around windows, woodland gardens filled
> with daffodils, ferns, and enormous white, fragrant lilies.
> She had a 120-foot-long, 20-foot-deep perennial border
> that went from pale, cool blues, to pinks, to apricots, to yel-
> lows, to reds, and back to cool colors again as you went down
> the path. . . . Really gorgeous stuff.
>
> She never had just one of anything. She had at least a
> dozen and probably eighty-five. She had a great eye, a real
> talent, and a staff of expert gardeners. She was rich. Her fam-
> ily had money.[3]

---

3 Cassandra Danz, *Mrs. Greenthumbs: How I Turned a Boring Yard into a Glorious Garden and How You Can, Too* (New York: Crown Publishers, 1993).

By now you're probably wondering, *How on earth did you get to see her private journals where all her secrets were stored?* I'll tell you. It was probably the highlight of my trip, even overshadowing three different theater shows on London stages.

I discovered an unassuming but charming little museum called the Museum of Garden History.[4] And quite frankly, you should donate money to it. It's touted as the first museum in the world dedicated to gardeners and gardening. Inside is a fascinating collection of antique tools, early lawn mowers, seeds, and gorgeous gardening books—which you can enjoy along with a cup of tea, if you like. You'll also find stationery, tea towels, and even note cards with Prince Charles's watercolors on them (quite good). He is the patron of this museum.

Along with this charming history and fascinating information about the history of gardening, the museum has a little section devoted to Gertrude Jekyll. They show her garden journals, which contain her color sketches illustrating where the color should go in a garden layout. Some of the plans were blown up and mounted on the wall so you can really pour over them. Her desk where she sat and wrote all this down is there too. I felt as if she had just stepped out to get something in the garden and would be back in a minute. Meanwhile, I pored over her notes.

I write another kind of journal that helps me along in this journey of life. My prayer journal. Like the gardening journal, the entries are straight from the hip and from the heart. I don't have to write in it every

---

4 Museum of Garden History, Lambeth Palace Road, London SE1 7LB.
  Web site: *www.museumgardenhistory.org.*

day, and I don't try to impress anyone—it's for my eyes only. I work through the issues in my life by letting loose before God in my journal with my praise, doubts, and frustrations. David sets a great example of this in the Psalms.

God said that David "was a man after my own heart." That's pretty astounding. Especially when you consider that David didn't hold anything back from God in his journal, the Psalms: "Will the Lord reject forever? Will he never show his favor again? Has his unfailing love vanished forever? Has his promise failed for all time? Has God forgotten to be merciful? Has he in anger withheld his compassion?" (Psalm 77:7–9). David didn't always laud God with glorious compliments. In this passage we see him doubting God's faithfulness and afraid of the future. I've felt that way many times, haven't you? In my prayer journal I've written,

God, I don't understand you. Everything looked like it was supposed to work and then it didn't. I hear nothing from you but silence. Frankly, I'm irritated. I don't expect you to do everything my way (although that would be nice!), but I *would* like to hear from you. Do I give up? Press on?

I'm thankful David wrote down his doubts so we could relate to him thousands of years later. He also recorded his wonder at God's handiwork. Again in the Psalms he writes, "The heavens declare the glory of God; the skies proclaim the work of his hands. Day after day they pour forth speech; night after night they display knowledge" (19:1–2). And in Psalm 147 David writes, "He sends his command to the earth; his word runs swiftly. He spreads the snow like wool and scatters the frost like ashes. He hurls down his hail like pebbles. Who can withstand his icy blast? He sends his word and melts them; he stirs up his breezes, and the waters flow" (1:15–18).

Keeping a record, an account, is important. Whenever God reveals something wonderful—or even something I did that was not so wonderful—my husband encourages me to write it down. If I write it down in my prayer journal, I will not forget it. If I write it down I can avoid the same mistake in the future. If I write it down I can recall the emotions, the insight I received. If I write it down I can refer back to my notes and see how God saw me through. If I write it down I won't get sucked down into the black hole of despair when all seems dark and there are no answers, because I can go back to the truth, the light that I have recorded. My prayer journal is like my garden journal; it's a compass or a road map to show me where I've been and where I'm going. So, too, is the written account of God's faithfulness toward us in the Bible.

Luke begins his account of Jesus' life and ministry by describing this very purpose:

Many have undertaken to draw up an account of the things that have been fulfilled among us, just as they were handed down to us by those who from the first were eyewitnesses and servants of the word. Therefore, since I myself have carefully investigated everything from the beginning, it seemed good also to me to write an orderly account for you, most excellent Theophilus, so that you may know the certainty of the things you have been taught (1:1–4).

So that you may know the certainty of the things you have been taught. That's why we should write it down. So we know; so we don't forget. Life has a way of stripping all God's promises from our memory. Promises about taking care of us and always being there with us, no matter how fierce the storm.

Paul's letters to the believers in Rome, Corinth, Ephesus, Philippi, and Colossus were all about documenting and remembering God's love, grace, and faithfulness to them and to us today—despite the conditions that surround us. Because, as those believers and we ourselves demonstrate, we are too quick to forget. Thank God it's written down, so we can look back and be reminded as we step into the future. As Psalm 119:105 states, "Thy word is a lamp to my feet, And a light to my path" (NASB).

Growing Points

1. What is your favorite psalm? Why? (If you don't have one, choose one.)

2. Recall and write down a specific event or time in your life when you felt God was trying to teach you something.

3. What biographies or stories have you read that helped you to face situations in life?

4. If you could write a letter to God, what would you say?

Staking

I was a voracious reader in childhood. Being sent to my room was a delicious punishment, because then I could read for hours undisturbed. One book had a scene I'll always remember. Two people were shipwrecked on a little island. A horrific hurricane blew up, and to survive, the two tied themselves to a big palm tree. The palm tree bent over to the ground, but it didn't break. Everything they had was blown off the island. But because they were strapped to the tree, they survived. I think about that scene every once in a while when a plant of mine needs to be staked.

The afternoon "breeze" (I'd call it wind) picks up in our area around one o'clock in the afternoon. It blows from east to west, and during a storm, if my tree roses aren't staked securely, the wind blows them down to the ground. Many plants fare much better with a little support.

The first plants I ever saw staked were my father's tomato plants, next to the old swing set in our backyard. Before then, I hadn't known anything about growing tomatoes. As they began to grow taller and sag under the weight of the developing fruit, I saw the necessity of staking them. Without support, the plants would slump to the ground where the fruit would fall prey to all sorts of bugs. Even without bugs, the tomatoes would rot quickly while resting on the ground. My father solved this problem with wire tomato cages around each plant.

Besides tomatoes, other plants benefit from some support.[1] My tree roses need support too. A tree rose is just a rosebush that's been trained to grow like a miniature tree. They are also called *standards*. These rose-bushes grow on top of a stalk or trunk that is about thirty-six inches tall. If you don't like to bend over much, tree roses are easier to take care of than regular rosebushes. To stake my tree roses, I do what most garden-ers do. I drive a stake (about two inches by two inches) into the ground within four to six inches of the trunk. Near the top of the stake I tie the stake to the tree rose using a figure eight loop, crisscrossing between the two so as not to chafe the trunk of the tree rose. You don't need to lash it tightly. The object is to give it some support when a strong wind blows through. However, a visiting rose guru stopped by one day and informed me I really should have *two* stakes—one on each side of the tree rose—to give them even more support. At the rate he was charging per hour I decided to do it myself, so of course, I still haven't gotten to it yet.

Delphiniums are aristocratic, sky blue—and frustrating for me. I adore their color. I admire their majestic spires. I loathe their tendency to topple over at the slightest breeze. I wouldn't mind if they gave me sev-

---

[1] Gardener's Supply catalog has a great selection of plant supports (888-833-1412 or *www.gardeners.com*).

eral flushes of bloom throughout the summer like my roses do. But delphiniums give me one gorgeous moment of color in midspring and then topple over. I faithfully tried staking them for a couple of years, but I finally gave up. I'm a bargain hunter. If a plant is only going to give me one good bloom, forget about it. I have other plants that are more rewarding, such as dahlias.

I grin every time I launch into how fabulous dahlias are, because I didn't like them at first. As I mentioned earlier, I thought they were too common, too garish. I was into roses, I was into scents, I was into *romance*. I still enjoy those aspects of gardening, but now I'm also into practicality. I enjoy a plant that gives me masses of blooms all summer long. I admire a plant that lasts forever in a vase. I take pleasure in a plant that comes in a zillion different shapes and colors. I now like dahlias.

What first attracted me to dahlias was my sister's rapture whenever she talked about them. She would go on and on about how great they were. Then I noticed all the lovely colors and forms they came in. When I saw a huge dinner-plate-sized dahlia, I couldn't resist! The first one I planted was a soft pink variety called Katsuga, and it *was* just as big as a dinner plate. Whether it was in the garden or in a vase inside, people would point and ask, "What is *that* flower?" Unfortunately, the slugs and snails were thrilled about it too. And when the giant heads got too heavy, they sank down to the ground. Then they became a delectable dessert for my slimy invaders. So I learned the value of staking them. Sometimes I use round tomato cages, and sometimes I use just a regular wooden stake. It doesn't take much to support them, and they reward my small effort by pumping out continuous flowers all summer long and into the fall.

Just as some plants do better with a little support, so do people. In the United States many of us are infected with a can-do attitude. This probably comes from the Revolutionary War days. We pride ourselves on being self-reliant, up-by-my-own-bootstraps people. People who make it on their own, who claim they don't need anybody else, are treated with respect in our society. But God made us relational people, first with Him and then with others. Throughout the Bible God gives us examples to show it's not only okay to get a little support now and then, but it's also part of His design.

Even though God told Moses, "I will help you speak and will teach you what to say," Moses was still too chicken to take on the job of being God's spokesman and leader of the people. He responded, "O Lord, please send someone else to do it" (see Exodus 4:12–17). Despite Moses' lack of faith, God provided the support Moses thought he needed through Moses' brother, Aaron.

When I read the account of Pentecost—when the disciples were filled with fearless power and witnessing muscle—it's natural to assume they were so strong after this event that they never needed their faith to be bolstered. That isn't so. In Acts 14 we read that Barnabas and Paul "preached the good news in that city and won a large number of disciples. Then they returned to Lystra, Iconium and Antioch, *strengthening the disciples and encouraging them to remain true to the faith*" (vv. 21–22). I find that fascinating. After seeing thousands of people converted throughout the area, the other disciples still needed to be encouraged (strengthened and supported) to remain true to the faith. Just like we are, they were subject to doubt, fears, and turning back.

This ministry of encouragement or support also shows up in the book of Hebrews. "But encourage one another daily, as long as it is called Today, so that none of you may be hardened by sin's deceitfulness" (3:13). And "Let us not give up meeting together, as some are in the habit of doing, but let us encourage one another—and all the more as you see the Day approaching" (10:25). Even Jesus desired encouragement and support in His darkest hour. He pleaded with the disciples in the Garden of Gethsemane, "My soul is overwhelmed with sorrow to the point of death. Stay here and keep watch with me" (Matthew 26:38). Clearly, we are called to support and strengthen one another.

Just as we give support to our plants to help them be more fruitful or show off their blooms better, we are to encourage and support one another in order to glorify God. Romans 1:11–12 says, "I long to see you so that I may impart to you some spiritual gift to make you strong—that is, that you and I may be mutually encouraged by each other's faith."

Seeking support doesn't mean you are weak. It means you care more about seeing God's glory displayed than you care about winning the bootstrap award. It means you don't mind identifying with Jesus. In Matthew 20:26–28, He said, "Whoever wants to become great among you must be your servant, and whoever wants to be first must be your slave—just as the Son of Man did not come to be served, but to serve, and to give his life as a ransom for many."

When we serve and support others, we are helping them to bloom and be fruitful. We are acting as Jesus would. And that's the whole point of our short time on earth.

Growing Points

1. Who has given you support in the past?

2. How did Jesus serve or support people during His earthly ministry?

3. What things did the disciples do to serve and support others?

4. Whom do you know that you could stand alongside, like a stake for support?

Born-Again Rose

"Take it!" my sister said in exasperation. "It's obviously dead. I was ripped off by that stupid catalog." She thrust the brown, dried, stick thing that was supposed to be a rosebush into my hands.

"You never know," I said. "Maybe it *does* have life in it." When rosebushes are thirty-five dollars at the nursery, you don't say no to a free one; you say thank-you.

The rose had a sumptuous name with great promise, Souvenir de la Malmaison, named after the empress Josephine's house and gardens at Versailles. She had spent years collecting and gathering the finest roses from all over the world for her rose garden. Since I was, and still am, an obsessed rose addict, this fact endeared her to me.

The catalog promised that the rose would have a color of the softest baby-cheek pink and would bloom like a many-petaled cabbage rose, with a fragrance that would make people stop to find out which rose was emanating that heavenly scent. All this sounded like heaven to me (and it was free) so I took it home with high hopes.

I found a protected spot against the house to plant it. I gave it a generous hole filled with well-rotted horse manure. The sun reflected off the cream color of the house. I kept the soil moist. The rose still looked bad. No promising nodules of future branches appeared. My other roses were well into spring, leafing out and starting to set buds. This one showed no such promise. But I was determined to leave it to its own timetable. When it was ready, it would start—if there was any life left in its roots.

Don't you wish people would treat you the same way when you're going through tough times? Just give you some space in the sun, protected, safe and warm, knowing that when the time is right (or you've finally decided that you'll listen to God) you'll blossom?

I was in a Bible study one Wednesday afternoon with many senior (and some downright elderly) ladies. We had been studying Proverbs 22:6—"Train a child in the way he should go, and when he is old he will not turn from it." Many of them were lamenting that, despite their training, their children or their grandchildren appeared to be on the express train for hell—or at least to a ruined life. No evidence of the life of God could be seen in these loved ones; how discouraging and futile it all seemed. Many times I had wondered why I was in that odd little Bible study, with nobody near my age, nobody I could really bond and kvetch with. But now I knew.

I stood up and said, "You all probably look at me and assume that I'm a nice Christian woman who is faithful to show up at this Bible study. But if you were to look at me in my college years, and on and off through the years after school, you would have thought I had no desire for the things of God—despite being raised in a family where we went to church every Sunday. There was no evidence in my life. I was goofing off, wasting my talents, and to all outside appearances, on the fast track to nowhere. But many times, late at night, I would talk to God. I would cry out to God. There was always this hole in my heart, and I knew that eventually I'd fill it by getting close to Him. Years later, I put my trust in Jesus—what some people call being born again. So don't assume that what you see on the outside is what is happening on the inside. Keep praying; there *is life* in there! Don't be discouraged and don't give up on them,'cause, hey, look at me! Who would have thought I would end up here with *you* guys?" Flushed red with embarrassment, I abruptly sat down.

The teacher cleared her throat and said something like: "Thank you for sharing. Now let's move on." I wondered if I had blown it with these sweet ladies. The truth was out: I wasn't the perfect, sweet Christian woman that they probably were—or thought themselves to be. I wondered if the warm acceptance I had always enjoyed from them would cool now that they knew my past. I have a tendency to put not merely my foot in my mouth, but my whole leg as well, and I wondered if this was one of those grand feasts. My father's frequent advice to "not open my mouth and remove all doubt" was echoing in my memory.

The shame was short-lived. Afterward, several women came up to me, placed their soft, gnarled hands in mine and whispered, "Thank you." The relief and hope in their eyes spoke volumes. I was glad I had taken the risk and shared. Maybe a few less critical eyes would be cast toward wayward souls struggling to find their way. Maybe a few less life-or-death judgments would be rendered so quickly.

Every time I walk by the side of the house and gaze affectionately at my Souvenir de la Malmaison rose, I remember that day at the Bible study and reflect on my own life. To all outside appearances, this rose had died. You'd never know that looking at it today. It is a sumptuous feast of fragrance and beauty, seven feet tall and laden with gorgeous blossoms. I relish burying my nose deep into its soft interior to inhale its glorious fragrance. All it needed was some patience and tender lovin' care. Visitors to my garden often ask me about *that* rose. And to think it was mistaken for dead, headed for the trash heap.

Growing Points

1. ❦ Was there a time in your life when your outward appearance lacked evidence of a Christian life inside you? Recall a few details of that time.

2. ❦ Read John 13:36–38; 18:15–27; and 21:1–19. What character traits does Peter demonstrate in these verses?

3. ❦ How did Jesus respond to Peter after his denial? What does this tell you about how we should respond to people after they fail?

4. ❦ Have you met anyone who said they "believed in God" or "were a Christian" but didn't act like it? How did you first respond when you saw their behavior?

~

I'm not one of those people you'll see in a worship service exclaiming how thunderstruck I am. In fact, I have trouble not comparing my experience with those who are swaying with their arms toward heaven, tears running down their faces in ecstasy. I'm either comparing my lack of a glorious experience with theirs, resulting in jealousy, or I end up doubting their sincerity and intellect. This attitude, of course, is not conducive to drawing closer to God. Therefore, because of these distractions, I usually have my *aha!* glimpses-of-heaven moments when I'm alone.

Many years ago I was feeling extremely low, disgusted with myself and my behavior. My life felt like a garden that was overgrown with big nasty weeds. An ugly mess. I had met with a kindly, older Christian woman counselor to sort out my head. She suggested that I had a problem with guilt. *Guilt?* I thought. *She's nuts!* I had enough theology during all my years of Bible study to know that I was saved by the sacrifice of Jesus, washed in the blood, my sins were laid on Him, and there was "therefore now no condemnation." But I was to discover the giant chasm between my head and my heart. The distance in my body is about eighteen inches, but in the spiritual realm, it can rival the size of the Grand Canyon. And sometimes it takes a small miracle to cross that chasm.

So there I was, moping around my apartment, feeling the Holy Spirit urging me to sit down and talk with God. *I'm sick of praying and reading,* I argued with myself. *If I have to read one more "how to be a better Christian" book, I'm going to scream.* But like a gentle, persistent knocking, came this call to sit down and face what God might want to say to me. I didn't want to sit down with my Bible, fishing around endlessly for some verse that might speak to me, so I grabbed *The Jesus Person Pocket Promise Book.* It's a wonderful little book that is filled with the promises of God. It takes care of the "hunting and fishing" aspect when you want some immediate encouragement or promise from God. *Hmm, she thinks I need to work on guilt,* I thought as I turned the pages to find some verses on guilt.

Who dares accuse us whom God has chosen for his own? Will God? No! He is the one who has forgiven us and given us right standing with himself. Who then will condemn us? Will Christ? *No!* For he is the one who died for us and came back to life again for us and is sitting at the place of highest honor next to God, pleading for us there in heaven. (Romans 8:33–34 TLB).

Right then I had one of those rare, breathless, glimpses-of-heaven moments. Even though I had been a Christian for many years and had read this passage before, it was like the fog had lifted. I saw into another realm. The veil parted. Or, as my friends in Australia say, *the penny dropped.* A tremendous "clink" sounded as my head knowledge dropped into my heart.

I'm sort of at a loss for words with which to describe it, other than my eyes were truly opened. I sobbed for about two hours in awe, in gratefulness, and in joy.

When other people tell me of their experiences or personal revelations with Scripture, I'm not particularly moved. Not that the event isn't wonderful; it's just that what moves them doesn't move me. I'm not struggling with the same things they are. Certain passages will make me think, *Wow! I never realized how much this applies to me.* But you might think, *Yeah, I know that already—no big deal.* I like this, because it demonstrates to me that God knows where our hearts are and His Word is truly "living and active. Sharper than any double-edged sword" (Hebrews 4:12).

This week I'm in a Bible study that is studying the Romans passage that gave me my glimpse of heaven years ago. And, as usual, it's amazing how I am getting the opportunity to apply what I am studying.

The children's book *Alexander and the Terrible, Horrible, No Good, Very Bad Day* describes what my last few days have been like. To start off, it's been

raining, and our bathroom ceiling is falling in, literally. When the roofer
came to inspect it, he pulled a little at the soaking wet ceiling, making it
give way in big, messy clumps onto my nearly new carpeting. And then, a
big fat *possum* fell down at our feet! I don't know who was more shocked,
the possum or us. (I made the roofer usher Mr. Possum outside.) Add to
that charming episode a busy schedule, and I've been grumpy to the point
of nasty. I've been angry at my lack of organization and weepy and frustrated over the seemingly insurmountable amount of work to be done.
I've been struggling with constant, negative self-talk. (*You'll never get your act
together—look at the mess you're in. You'll never change. You haven't changed an iota since
becoming a Christian—a lot of good that's done you!*) It's been a terrible, horrible,
no good, very bad week.

After my husband and I had an argument, we sat down to talk about
what brought me to this miserable state of mind and how to get out of it.
Sometimes the obvious isn't so obvious when you are sitting in a dark
hole. He asked me if I was having my daily quiet times (ouch). No, I
wasn't. "Too busy" was my reply, which I knew was a stupid excuse. He
asked me what sort of negative things I was telling myself. "Oh, that I'm
hopeless, that life isn't fair, that I'll never get my act together," I said. He
asked, "And *who* do you think is putting those thoughts into your head
and wants you to feel this way?" I knew it wasn't my Lord, who had just
told me through Romans 8 how much He was *for* me. A distinct image of
Dana Carvey from *Saturday Night Live* doing his Church Lady skit came to
mind. Although Carvey pokes fun at constipated, holier-than-thou
Christians, he's quite funny. He dresses like a dowdy spinster, purses his

lips in a disapproving way, and asks rhetorically, "And *who* could that be? Satan?" Yes, I was listening to the enemy of my soul and buying all his lies.

In my yard I'm never surprised to see weeds develop—they are a normal occurrence in gardens. So I don't know why I'm so surprised and depressed when they appear in my spiritual life. All it takes for weeds to gain a strong foothold in the garden is a little bit of inattentiveness. They are so small at first that I don't pay much attention. *I'll get to those in a couple of days*, I think as I pass by them with my morning coffee. After a couple of days with fabulous growing conditions (a little sun, a little rain), I return to find some monster weeds with roots that seem to reach down to the earth's inner core. It's amazing how what you *don't* want to grow in your garden can take off like Jack's beanstalk, and what you've spent good money on and fussed over can sulk and creep along. But that's the way it is.

And that's the way it is in my spiritual life. I can blow off reading my Bible and talking to God for a couple of days, thinking, *Oh, I'm busy, He knows I love Him. I'll get back to Him later—no big deal.* Meanwhile, some conditions sprout that are conducive to stress and misery. People become obnoxious and annoy me, I have less and less time to get things done, while more and more responsibilities and deadlines pile onto me, and then I'm wondering five days later why I'm in such a foul place. What I *want* to grow in me is a more Christlike character, but what seems to germinate and grow quickly is my nasty human nature.

Sometimes I get frustrated that things deteriorate so easily. I'm amazed that the afterglow of my glimpses-of-heaven moments don't carry me through life forever. Like the grumbling Israelites following Moses, I too, quickly forget. Instead, I find myself having to reweed areas in my spiritual life. I find myself facing the same lesson many times over.

Weeding can be a very satisfying pastime. Digging my fingers deep into the soil, grabbing the root at its base and yanking it out of my rose garden fills me with a wonderful sense of accomplishment. It's mindless work that allows me to be mindful. Mindful that while those glimpses-of-heaven moments are wonderful, they do not mean I'll never have to pass this way again. Even the apostle Paul said that he struggled. "I do not understand what I do. For what I want to do I do not do, but what I hate I do" (Romans 7:15). As I'm down on my knees weeding, I remind myself that this is an ongoing process. (I accidentally typed "ongroping process" at first, which I think is closer to the truth.) This is comforting, because when that lesson swings back around again years later, I can avoid beating myself up. Everybody is "groping" through this process called sanctification. There will always be some weeding to do.

It's surprising to me that the big moments in life rarely account for my eyes being opened. Most of the time the common, repetitive "weed-ing," the daily upkeep of applying God's Word to my recurring sins, addictions, and discouraging times results in the eye-opening moments. Then I can be transformed by the renewing of my mind with the truth. The weeding clears the way for my eyes to be opened, for my faith to blos-som and flourish. And that's what I call God's gardening mercies, a glimpse of heaven.

Growing Points

1. ✧ What "weeds" are common in your life? In your attitude? In your behavior?

2. ✧ Recall a time when God revealed to you a verse that opened your eyes, was meaningful for your situation, or gave you a glimpse of heaven.

3. ✧ What things can you do to prevent "weeds" from choking out your inner garden?

4. ✧ What's the best way to take care of "weeds" in your life once they have taken root?

Self-Sowers

Just after Christmas is one of my favorite times of the year. All the seed and plant companies stuff my mailbox with colorful catalogs promising gardening glories. I consider it absolute bliss to sit down with a hot drink in front of a crackling fire and peruse those catalogs. I used to do this in bed before going to sleep, but then I'd toss and turn all night envisioning new plants and ideas for the garden. While I sit by the fire with a rainstorm pounding down around the house, I try to remember what colors are where in the garden and what needs to be replaced. My yearly wintertime ritual also has an amusing side: I find deciphering the descriptions of the plants a challenge.

You need to read the catalog descriptions the way you read want ads—with an eye toward what is *not* stated. When they say "subtle scent," what they really mean is that a bloodhound would have a tough time discerning anything close to a fragrance emanating from this flower. Get it for the color or form, but don't expect a fragrance.

"Give it room" means you'll be amazed at how that squash plant can spread twenty to thirty feet and start to take over the neighborhood. It also might mean that you will spend every spring digging out this plant's invasive roots so that it doesn't smother your other plants.

"Eye-catching color" means you'll need sunglasses every time you walk by that ghastly Day-Glo orange. It will be a color normally not found in nature, sure to be seen from hundreds of yards away—like the bright orange cones warning you of highway construction. And "self-sows readily" means in every crack of the driveway and patio, in every two-inch bit of soil, and in your dried-out birdbath, this plant will self-sow vigorously, or "show up." Sometimes that's a good thing.

If you pick a plant that you like and you're short on time, a self-sower can be like manna from heaven. A hundred plants for the price of one! Once I ordered White Wonder from the Cook's Garden catalog.[1] The Latin name is *Matricaria capensis* or *T. parthenium*, more commonly known as feverfew. It's kind of like baby's breath on growth hormones. About two feet tall, the plants are covered with masses of small, white pomponlike flowers that are bigger than baby's breath and smaller than bachelor's buttons. Feverfew is the ultimate garden filler. It will grow in full sun, shade—anywhere it can find a smidgen of soil. Plus, it looks great at twilight, like waves of billowing white frothiness. People always ask me what it is and comment on my landscaping skills. I don't let on that it's God orchestrating the wind, the birds, and the bees to spread this plant.

---

[1] The Cook's Garden catalog (800-457-9703 or *www.cooksgarden.com*) offers great vegetables too.

I like people to think I artfully arranged it all. However, it *is* a massive self-sower. So if you don't mind it showing up several places in the garden, it's a great little investment.

Other prolific self-sowers are alyssum (*Lobularia maritima*—a small ground-cover-like version of baby's breath), forget-me-nots (*Myosotis*—delicate, tiny, sky-blue flowers), foxglove (*Digitalis*—tall flowers, like delphiniums in pastel colors), flowering tobacco (*Nicotiana alata*), and sweet William (*Dianthus barbatus*—sweet-smelling pink to red colors). Right now Jupiter's-beard (*Centranthus*) is spreading like gossip around my garden. It has deep pink flowers (it also comes in white) and despite the catalog's description—"avoid heavy clays!"—it is quite prolific in my clay soil. I never even planted it. My neighbor across the street has it and now I do too. That tells you something about the strength of some of these self-sowers.

Some annuals self-sow like crazy too. The ones I'm happy about are spiderflower (*Cleome spinosa*—four- to five-feet tall with pink and white flowers that look like spiders or spiky mums) and hollyhocks (*Alcea rosea*—tall, old-fashioned plants bearing single or double flowers the full length of the stalk. Most charming behind picket fences). My sister says, "Once you have hollyhocks, you'll *always* have hollyhocks."

It's fascinating to me how you have to baby some plants and prod them along, constantly monitoring and encouraging their progress. Others reproduce effortlessly to provide you with duplicates all over your garden.

My husband's mother, Dorothy Kehler, is a self-sower. Ever since Tom can remember, his mother's home has been open to everyone. Visiting friends, confused youths, missionaries on break, and soldiers on furlough all find a welcome spot at the table and a place to lay their heads. No matter how big the crowd, Dorothy drops everything. She's always ready to serve encouraging words and one of her famous pies. As a result, people are drawn to this God of hers who distributes His love and acceptance so freely.

My mother, Helen Ostby, is also a self-sower. Some of my earliest memories of childhood are of watching her teach blind children how to swim. She's always the first one to welcome a new neighbor with some food. At the age of sixty-two, when most women are taking it easy, she fielded emergency phone calls for her community's *First Call for Help* phone lines. She's set a great example to me by serving at the local nursing home and inviting friends to church.

We don't have to be Superwoman or Betty Crocker for God to use us. It helps me to remember that God can and will use *any* situation. We don't have to try to engineer it or control things. For example, my friend Simon has a personal trainer. During the treadmill portion of his workout. Simon has been watching a video about the life of Jesus. Thus, his trainer is forced to watch it too. Simon's trainer is a woman with a New Age background who knows nothing about church or the Bible. But she has become interested since watching this video with him and is asking Simon some questions. She even asked him, "So if I *were* to get a Bible to read, which one do you recommend?" (Simon suggested the *Life Applica-*

tion Study Bible.) Simon is not a natural evangelist. In fact, he's quite shy. All he did in this situation was live his life the way he usually does. He showed up and he switched on a video. God took care of the rest.

I don't go out of my way to evangelize. I'm too shy. I pray for people and for God to open up opportunities for me to help them. He's amazingly good at that. Sometimes it's as simple as sharing with someone about my daily life. When someone asks me to a meeting on Wednesday mornings, I could say, "Uh, I'm busy then." Or I could say, "I'm sorry, I can't make it then. That's the time of my weekly Bible study." If they want to know more, they can ask. Some do, some don't. The important thing is not how much you know, but how *available* you are for God to use you in someone else's life.

Just being available resulted in God's using me in a most unexpected way. My neighbor had a brother who was gay and suffering with full-blown AIDS. I had only met him once. He was trimming her Japanese maple and I was watching him and taking notes. After I shook his hand and thanked him for the lesson, I turned toward home and thought, *Lord, I'll probably never see him again and there's nothing I can do for him. He most likely doesn't want to talk to you, but I can pray for him. I can pray that he would discover your peace.* It was one of those quickie, shoot-up-to-heaven prayers that you say and then soon forget.

Weeks later, my neighbor (I'll call her Margaret) told me with tears that her brother was in the hospital, dying. She said, "He won't talk to a pastor, a priest, *nobody!* I'm so worried about his eternal future!"

"Margaret," I said, "*you* can talk to him about God; *you* can lead him to salvation. I'll give you a sheet of paper; just read it to him." So I went back home and wrote out the steps to receiving Jesus and eternal life with Him. I kept it to a simple, one-page explanation.[2] Frankly, I didn't know where *she* stood with the Lord, so I figured it could serve more than one purpose.

Days later Margaret knocked on my door. "You won't believe what happened! My mother and I were in his hospital room. I said to her, '*You* read it to him, Mom.' My mother said, 'No, *you* read it,' and back and forth we went. So finally I sat down with him and read it through. When I got to the question about wanting to receive Jesus into his heart, he couldn't speak anymore because he was so dehydrated, but he nodded his head and squeezed my hand. He did it! The next day he died—but he did it!"

I was blown away. The enormity of what had transpired in the heavenlies left me awed. Here was a guy who probably had been told by most Christians that he was an abomination to God. And consequently, anything to do with the church was anathema to him. Yet, just because I was available, God bridged a giant gulf between His heart of love and an estranged child of His. All I did was show up.

---

[2] A copy of what my neighbor read to her dying brother appears in the appendix.

It didn't stop there, either. At the man's funeral, the pastor told of what had happened in that hospital room and read aloud the Scriptures I had put together on that sheet of paper for Margaret. So the message of how to receive Christ was then told to a whole congregation of people. God took my small, solitary response to Margaret and multiplied it tenfold.

When Jesus picked out the fishermen Simon (Peter) and Andrew to be disciples, He didn't say, "Oh, first you must go study. Go to seminary. Become expert theologians." No, He just wanted them to be available. They were fishermen, and Jesus didn't want to change their skills. He simply said to them, "Follow Me, and I will make you fishers of men" (Matthew 4:19 NASB). You don't need any particular skill to become a natural self-sower. You just need to be available. God will take care of the rest. He will make sure His seeds are sown in others' hearts.

Growing Points

I. ❧ Who do you know that is a natural self-sower, spreading love around to others?

2. ❧ Who do you run into on a daily basis (neighbors, people you encounter while doing errands, etc.) that you could pray for?

3. ❧ What talents or abilities do you have that you could use to serve others (like Dorothy's cooking)?

4. ❧ Read 2 Corinthians 9:6–15. What does this teach you about sowing?

The group of ladies quieted down as the elderly woman struggled to rise from her chair. We were attending a woman's conference on spiritual growth, and women of all ages were there. She must have been in her early eighties, I surmised. She was dressed elegantly; everything matched and not a hair was out of place. I was sitting behind her and could see her crepe-paper skin draw taut when she gripped the back of her chair for support. Her other hand fluttered unsteadily to her throat as she cleared it and tilted her head to speak. "So what you're telling me," she asked the speaker in the quavering voice of the elderly, "is that our @#$% is our fertilizer?"

A stunned silence hung in the air. Then an outburst of laughter. How funny and shocking to hear that word come out of an eighty-year-old woman's mouth! But she got straight to the point. Yes, the tough times in our lives, our worst struggles with our flesh, all our mistakes, are our fertilizer—our compost. It's what God uses to help us grow to be more like His Son. Catherine Marshall said it more poetically in her book,

Something More: "Our God is the Divine Alchemist. He can take junk from the rubbish heap of life, and melting this base refuse in the pure fire of His love, hand us back gold."

Nothing is wasted in God's economy and that's a principle we can use in our gardens.

Composting is not new; it's been around as long as human beings. Composting was probably first understood when people noticed that plants grew better next to rotting piles of vegetation and manure. References to composting are found in medieval church texts and Renaissance literature. Printer William Caxton wrote about "compostyng." In literature, Shakespeare's *Hamlet* says, "Do not spread the compost on the weeds, to make them ranker."

Composting as we know it, in the twenty-first century, is credited to Sir Albert Howard. He was a British government agronomist who went to India for twenty-nine years and experimented with different approaches to composting. He settled on an approach called the Indore Method. This method calls for three parts plant material to one part manure, with materials spread in layers and turned during decomposition. Howard felt so strongly about composting and taking care of the soil that he said, "Fertility of the soil is the future of civilization." J. I. Rodale, from the United States, is credited with making organic gardening and composting popular today.

Rodale formed the Farming Research Center and *Organic Farming and Gardening* magazine (later to be called *Organic Gardening*) in 1942 with Sir Albert Howard as one of the editors.

Today *Organic Gardening* magazine[1] is still going strong and now has a column called "Compost Corner." Each month it features a picture of a reader's compost pile and a description of how it was done. To every contributor, *Organic Gardening* sends out a "nifty pin." It's amazing how many different composting methods are used. Most people just carry out the kitchen scraps to a pile of leaves and grass clippings and give it a turn once in a while. But one woman had a heavy-duty garbage disposal with a diverter valve installed in her kitchen. So instead of sending her kitchen scraps to the sewage system, she diverted it outside through a downspout into a waiting bucket. She then took that bucket and poured it on her pile of leaves and other dry matter.

My sister has a lot of acreage so she has room for three huge bins for her ongoing composting piles. Into those bins she throws plants that have died or that she doesn't like anymore—grass clippings, leaves, scraps from the kitchen (never meat), and chicken and horse manure. She doesn't follow a prescribed amount of any material; she just tosses it all in. Because she has so much manure from her five horses, she doesn't have any problems with the pile heating up fast and decomposing quickly.

The two essential parts needed for compost are high-protein wastes

---

[1] *Organic Gardening* magazine (800-666-2206) has a tremendous Web site: *www.organic-gardening.com.*

and energy-rich materials. High-protein wastes include green vegetation (which provide nitrogen for the microorganisms that break down the compost) such as fresh grass clippings, recently pulled weeds, flowers, kelp, and kitchen scraps. Kitchen scraps include fruit skins, peels, and cores, vegetable parts, tea leaves, coffee grounds, stale bread, and non-meat leftovers. Animal manure is also considered a high-protein composting ingredient and should come from cow, chicken, or horse—never dogs or cats. Meat, oil and grease attract animals and should never be used in the pile.

Energy-rich materials are brown ingredients (that provide carbon, which is a food source for microorganisms). This group includes old leaves, flowers, grass clippings, paper towels, and straw.

For a compost pile to work, it needs to heat up enough to cause the materials to break down—to decompose. This heat and decomposing process kills off the unwanted weed seeds, breaks down all the plant and manure matter to an unrecognizable state, and turns it into a healthy loam. This loam, or compost, provides the perfect soil amendment for growth.

When God allows the heat to be turned up in our lives, it causes our independence and our arrogance to decompose—to break down. For decomposition to happen, there needs to be heat. God has a unique way of allowing situations into our lives that will reduce us to be fit for His use and for His glory to be displayed in our lives. In Isaiah 48:10–11, He says, "See, I have refined you, though not as silver; I have tested you in the furnace of affliction. For my own sake, for my own sake, I do this. How can I let myself be defamed? I will not yield my glory to another."

For a couple of years Tom was the single parent of three teenagers. He was overwhelmed at times, being in charge of doctor's appointments, sporting events, schooling, and meals. But through this humbling experience he was able to a grow a much closer and deeper relationship with his children than he ever had before. Out of a tragic experience, one which Tom did *not* want to be in, the heat was turned up and God grew beautiful relationships.

A friend of mine had an abortion at a young age. She now is involved with her local pregnancy care center, where she helps frightened girls who are in the same situation she was in. Because of her past mistakes she understands and identifies with these frightened women. God has taken her past heartbreak and spun it into a golden opportunity to reach out to others.

In the book of Romans, the apostle Paul writes, "And we know that in all things God works for the good of those who love him, who have been called according to his purpose" (8:28). Note the word *all* here. It means *all*, even the really horrible, sinful junk we can't tell anyone about. Therefore, we can have confidence that God uses our compost, the rubbish in our lives, to grow something good. But the key to this passage is *works for the good*. What "good"? Oftentimes our idea of what would be *good* and God's idea of *good* are worlds apart. *Good* doesn't mean the cushiest life possible for me. *Good* doesn't mean things going my way. The verse following Romans 8:28 shows us what *good* means to God. "For those God foreknew he also predestined to be conformed to the likeness of his Son." In God's definition, *good* means becoming more like Jesus Christ.

So how does all this sin and junk we've done to ourselves—or that's been done to us by others—turn into rich compost by which we can grow? How does it work for good, for us becoming more like Jesus?

It all hinges upon one little word—saying *yes* to God. We can say, "No, I won't stay in this tough situation with the heat building up. I'm getting out of here, I'm going to find someone to help me raise these kids. Forget it God—it's too painful." Or we can say yes with the attitude like Jesus had in the Garden of Gethsemane when He  said yes with clenched teeth and sweat pouring down: "Yet not what I will, but what *you* will" (Mark 14:36). Our yes, our surrender of our plans to God's plans, is a victory. In this day and age we don't like surrender. Surrender means failure, defeat. But not to God. Surrender to Him is victory for us. Jesus says, "Whoever loses his life for my sake will find it" (Matthew 10:39).

When we say yes to God's allowing the nasty situations of life, yes to His authority to use even our worst sins, yes to His sovereignty and power to work out the situation for good, we will find something new and beautiful growing in our hearts—the character of Jesus

Christ. The end of ourselves, the *yes* of surrender, is the beginning of God's transforming power. Saying yes to being thrown ignominiously onto the compost pile simply means that you're about to receive a huge dose of fertilizer. It doesn't always feel so great, it probably won't smell wonderful, but you have the promise of growth and all things working for your *good*.

Growing Points

1. What situation have you been in where you felt like God was turning up the heat and you were breaking down—decomposing?

2. What events in your life could be part of the "compost" that has caused you to grow?

3. In what areas of your life have you had to surrender—say yes—to God?

4. In what areas of your life are you seeing "all things working for the good"?

The Perfect Garden

Don't you love garden magazines and books? It's like entering another world when you turn those pages.

Here's a woman who lives in the South. She has a charming white picket fence that is covered with old-fashioned, romantic roses. Their pale pink, peony-sized blossoms in thick clusters climb up trellises and down to the street. Inside the fence it looks like the movie, *The Secret Garden*. Roses billow and spill over onto garden paths dotted with fragrant lavender.

Another article shows me a woman who lives in the country. Her garden is bursting with a riot of old-fashioned flowers. Hollyhocks, black-eyed Susans, and rainbow-colored zinnias line her fieldstone walkways next to her barn. Nearby in a field of poppies, her granddaughters are wearing straw hats and having a tea party under a cornflower-blue sky.

Whenever I see such picture-perfect gardens, I want to walk right into the pages and live there. Sometimes I'm even jealous. I wonder, *How can she get her plants to all look so perfect?!* It doesn't seem fair. I'm sure I work just as hard, and yet my garden is never that orderly. But I know things aren't always as they seem.

No matter how perfect and orderly those gardens are we see in books, magazines, and public gardens, I'll let you in on a secret. They are faking it. I know this because I used to work in advertising.

Whenever our agency oversaw a photo shoot for a product, we would make sure everything looked perfect. If a glass of milk needed to look frosty and inviting, we would put a gel-like substance, similar to rubbery glue, on the outside of the glass. That gave it an ice-cold, frosty look. The minute a piece of lettuce wilted under the hot lights, we would replace it with another, over and over again. Produce was misted with a product that beaded-up to make it look just-washed fresh. Lingerie models had their thighs, moles, and other imperfections caught on film altered on the computer to make themselves and the lingerie look better.

All this "image management" for perfection happens in garden photo shoots too. Every dead flower head is removed, so the whole plant looks as if it burst into bloom all at once. In your garden and mine, flowers come and go intermittently over several weeks. In the photographed garden,[1] every open space in the flower borders is filled in with a potted plant. They either bury the pot or take it out and plant it, but just the same, they fake it. Everything is trimmed and neatened like your garden

---

[1] Professional photography tip: Take photos of your garden in the soft light of early morning or in the warm tones of sunset. Never at midday with the sun beating down; the colors will be washed out.

would be, too, if you had a staff to help you.

In real gardens—yours and mine—weeds exist. Real gardens have plants die for no apparent reason. Real gardens don't grow all tidy and perfect; sometimes half the plant is in bloom, the other half bedraggled. Real gardens have plants that need to be staked for support, plants that have to be pruned to make room for others, and some plants that have to be ripped out and moved to other locations. Real gardens are not picture-perfect. That is a contrived, artificial look reserved for photo shoots and professional staffers who specialize in making things look good.

We should remember this when we look at another's "perfect" life. That just isn't a reality concerning the human condition. Nothing and nobody (except Jesus Christ) is perfect. It's good for us to remember when we see someone's life that looks perfect to us, things aren't always as they seem.

I remember a Bible study I attended when I was a new Christian. In walked this beautiful woman. She had naturally white-blonde, curly hair. It feathered softly around her exquisite, creamy porcelain face. Her figure was elegant. Not stick thin, and not an ounce of fat. She wore a soft blue cashmere outfit that perfectly complemented her delicate and stunning beauty. She was soft-spoken and nice. She was dating the handsomest guy in our group. I felt uncomfortable and unattractive in comparison. *Everything about her is perfect,* I said to myself, trying not to stare or be overcome by jealousy.

Then during the prayer time, she asked for prayer for her brother and herself. She began to talk about her brother being in jail and earlier years of incest between them. My jaw sagged open. Suddenly, I wouldn't trade places with her for anything in the world.

I think about that day whenever I see someone's life that on the outside looks perfect. They seem to have the perfect marriage, the perfect home, the perfect children, and they never struggle with their weight. But I know things aren't always as they seem. I know I'm not seeing the full story. And furthermore, I know better than to play the comparison game. My pastor, Walt Gerber, said something I wrote in the back of my Bible to memorize: "The recipe for misery is comparison." Comparison will make you feel miserable and so will the pursuit of the appearance of perfection. But it makes me wonder, why are we—especially Christians—so tempted to play the game of image management? Of making it appear as though everything is perfect? Why are we so afraid to be real?

One reason is fear of judgment. We know the story of Jesus and the woman at the well. We know that although she had been living with several men, He did not condemn her. And we know that when another "sinful" woman anointed Him with tears and expensive oil, He was not offended by her presence. But we also know if the town prostitute, wife-beater, alcoholic, homosexual, or drug-dealer came to our church service, he or she wouldn't be treated the way Jesus treated those people. We would be repelled, or at least keep our distance. This lack of grace is what keeps our masks on and the secular world out of the church.

In Philip Yancey's brilliant book, *What's So Amazing About Grace?*, he writes about this tendency of ours to put on a false religious front. In discussing the scene in John 8 in which a woman is caught in adultery, Yancey points out our distorted view of right and wrong versus what Jesus viewed as right and wrong.

> Jesus grants absolution: "Then neither do I condemn you.... Go now and leave your life of sin" (v. 11).
>
> Thus in a brilliant stroke Jesus replaces the two assumed categories, righteous and guilty, with two different categories: sinners who admit and sinners who deny. The woman caught in adultery helplessly admitted her guilt. Far more problematic were people like the Pharisees who denied or repressed guilt.[2]

Our human tendency is to appear as something we are not, to engage in image management. Faking it was a constant source of trouble for Jacob. He didn't trust God to come through on his promise that "the older will serve the younger" (Genesis 25:23), so he contrived birthrights

---

[2] Philip Yancey, *What's So Amazing about Grace?* (Grand Rapids, Mich.: Zondervan Publishing House, 1997), 182.

and blessings in his own way, without relying on God to come through. This Machiavellian attitude and pretense caused him a lifetime of trouble.

Faking his own religious power cost Moses the Promised Land (Numbers 20:2–12). David faked as if he had done nothing wrong with Bathsheba or to her husband, Uriah (2 Samuel 11:2–17). God is never fooled or impressed, and faking it always results in the loss of intimacy and real relationship with others and our God. It's a barrier to closeness and all the good things we desire from relationships.

Image management is not pleasing to God. For Ananias and Sapphira their biggest mistake was the pretense of having given everything away (Acts 5:1–10). It would've been fine if they had said, "We sold our land and gave *some* of the money to you." Instead, they faked it. They pretended they were more noble and giving than they really were. The popular attitude *Fake it till you make it* definitely didn't make it for them.

Jesus had some scathing and vicious words to say about the Pharisees. He called them hypocrites, blind guides, blind fools, whitewashed tombs, and snakes. With everyone else, especially sinners, He was kind and compassionate. Why was He so angry with the Pharisees? Because "Everything they do is done for men to see" (Matthew 23:5). The Pharisees cared more about image management and looking good (or holy) than being real.

True transformational power—the power to touch another's life in a meaningful way with compassion, understanding, and authority—comes from being real. The woman who massaged and anointed Jesus' feet with oil and her hair didn't waste time with image management. She was aware that every man in the room knew about her lifestyle. But she was so focused on Jesus, so caught up with adoring Him, that she ceased to care what others thought. Consequently, Jesus said about her, "I tell you the truth, wherever this gospel is preached throughout the world, what she has done will also be told, in memory of her" (Matthew 26:13).

Have you ever tried to get close to someone who "has it all together"? These people look and act as if everything in their lives is perfect, they have no problems or struggles. It's a monumental challenge to get close to someone such as this, and worse, it prevents the closeness and fellowship that we are meant to have with one another. I never want to share my thoughts with someone taken up with image management: They make me feel inferior and unclean. These people can fake it for a while, but they will never experience true intimacy and fellowship with their God or anyone else until they admit they are needy too.

Jesus didn't fake it. He was angry with the money changers in the temple. He was sorrowful: He wept over the death of a friend. He was scared and anguished in the Garden of Gethsemane. Although He knew why He was dying on the cross, He wasn't Mr. Stoic. "My God, my God, why have you forsaken me?" was his tortured cry. Jesus showed us how to be real in a world full of pretense.

One of my favorite children's stories about being real is from the book *The Velveteen Rabbit*.

"What is REAL?" asked the Rabbit one day, when they were lying side by side near the nursery fender, before Nana came to tidy the room. "Does it mean having things that buzz inside you and a stick-out handle?"

"Real isn't how you are made," said the Skin Horse. "It's a thing that happens to you. When a child loves you for a long, long time, not just to play with, but REALLY loves you, then you become Real."

"Does it hurt?" asked the Rabbit.

"Sometimes," said the Skin Horse, for he was always truthful. "When you are Real you don't mind being hurt."

"Does it happen all at once, like being wound up," he asked, "or bit by bit?"

"It doesn't happen all at once," said the Skin Horse. "You become. It takes a long time. That's why it doesn't often happen to people who break easily, or have sharp edges, or who have to be carefully kept. Generally, by the time you are Real, most of your hair has been loved off, and your eyes drop out and you get loose in the joints and very shabby. But these things don't matter at all, because once you are Real you can't be ugly, except to people who don't understand."[3]

---

3 Margery Williams, *The Velveteen Rabbit* (New York: Doubleday, 1958).

There's no such thing as the perfect garden or the perfect person or the perfect Christian. It's all a sham, image management. The best we can hope for is to be real for one another. The next time you see some-one who seems to have "the perfect life," the more important question is: Are they living a life of pretense? Or are they real?

Growing Points

1. Whom have you met who seemed to have the perfect life?

2. How did that make you feel?

3. In what areas of your life are you involved in image management, or faking it?

4. What are the reasons you are doing this? (Fear of rejection, wanting to impress others, etc.?)

Pruning

If there were a Purple Heart for self-pity, I would have earned it last Christmas. I was beyond boo-hoo, I was thoroughly bah-humbug.

My husband, Tom, who has never been sick in the seven years we've been married, was down with a horrific cold. He lay on the couch, weak and helpless, while I rushed around and prepared for a Christmas season I didn't want to celebrate. My father was battling cancer and my brother was getting a divorce. But what was really crushing me was that I had just failed my fifth attempt at getting pregnant through in vitro fertilization. Despair, misery, frustration, and anger—no, make that *fury*—at God were daily emotional battles.

Most of my prayer time involved my sobbing and imploring God to let my body do what it was created and meant to do, make and carry a child. Most discussions with Tom ended with my screaming out my fury and frustration with God. Most mornings were spent holding a bag of frozen peas to eyes that had swollen shut from crying.

People were kind; they sent me encouraging notes. Usually they gave me Scripture verses that I received with the sarcastic thought: *Nice words, but they obviously don't apply to my situation.* Going to church was an emotional minefield; babies were everywhere. Adorable, pink, cuddly babies in mothers' arms, while my arms wondered if they'd ever hold my little one. I gave up caring that I looked like Tammy Faye with mascara running everywhere and just sobbed openly. Every hymn and message seemed to mock me, and I responded in growing bitterness.

Praying, I knew, is what I should have been doing. But I had pounded on God's chest for months and years, and I felt as if He either didn't care or was callously torturing me. I was so consumed with what I didn't have, I was blind to the blessings I did have: good health, a strong marriage, and a loving family. I was too shell-shocked by the Job-like miseries that had overtaken me and my loved ones.

When her husband died, Joan Rivers described the darkness this way: "I was in a mood that would've had to lighten a bit to become merely black."

Now, three months later, nothing has really changed in my litany of woes. But the weather is changing, and I think I am changing too, slowly.

I've noticed that spring is arriving. Daffodils are blooming, and the fruit trees are starting to bud out in delicate blossoms of pink and white. The weather is warmer, and my garden is responding. This, of course, happens every year, but this year spring has brought me a delicious whisper of hope—hope that tough, cold seasons in our lives don't go on *forever*. (Even Siberia has a spring and summer season.) There is a thaw and a change. "Things change, this won't go on forever," I said to myself as I looked out the window at my neighbor's garden. Then I realized, "I really miss being out in the garden."

Gardening always has brought immense pleasure and joy to me. I watch and marvel at God's creative handiwork among my flowers. No matter how much or little I accomplish, I always come back to the house feeling better about life. My "Martha Stewart" next-door neighbor summed up the benefits of gardening by saying: "It's cheaper than therapy."

One unseasonably warm, sunny day, the rosebushes caught my attention. They were long ago in need of pruning. This was a job I should have started a month ago, and it was obvious I was behind. Roses should be trimmed in their dormant state, when all the leaves from summer and autumn have fallen off but no new growth has started yet on the branches (or "canes"). By the time I got to them, they were beyond little nubs of growing branches; they were fully leafing out.

The goal in pruning rosebushes is air. Cut off all the canes that have grown in toward the center to give it more air. You want to have your finished product look like a catcher's mitt waiting for a catch, but without the leather webbing in between the fingers. (I once heard the desired result described as an empty urn, but to me, that reminds me of death and cremation, and we are talking about encouraging *life* here. So think catcher's mitt.) If you don't eliminate all those inward growing canes, the bush will get clogged up with too much growth come midsummer. Instead of enjoying armloads of roses for your vases, you'll have to deal with all the diseases that are attacking your roses because of the lack of air in the plant's interior. Diseases like black spot, powdery mildew, and rust will spread greedily in that overgrown environment and disfigure and ruin your roses. Therefore, you're doing your bushes a favor by pruning out all this wayward growth so they can grow healthy.

Many of my rosebushes bring back fond memories because they are associated with wonderful events. The antique Boule de Neige-1867 white rose Tom gave me for our first anniversary. The pink Queen Elizabeth hybrid tea my neighbor gave me not long after we moved in. So I was feeling a bit of hesitation when I faced them with my sharp gardening shears.

My red and *very* elegant Christian Dior hybrid tea rose was growing like crazy. Big, healthy looking canes were charging into the bush's center. Many more were crisscrossing in the center as well. I hated to cut off all that exuberant growth. It looked so healthy and happy! But I knew what would happen if I didn't prune. Sigh. *Snip. Snip.* Big, eight-inch-long canes fell to the ground. I could just hear the poor thing whimpering. But as the gardener tending the garden, I knew it was for the best in the long run.

It's one thing to hear a familiar Bible passage and quite another thing to have hands-on experience. Jesus says in John 15:1–2, "I am the true vine, and my Father is the gardener. He cuts off every branch in me that bears no fruit, while every branch that does bear fruit he prunes so that it will be even more fruitful."

With every careful, thought-out, orchestrated snip of the shears, I thought about this verse. *Snip.* I wonder what this big cane represents in my life? My control-freak nature? *Snip.* I am not in control, neither is science. He is in control of whether or not I have children. *Snip.* I thought about my script for my life. *Snip.* My script is that my husband is wildly successful, makes lots of money (well, okay, just "abundantly beyond all that we could ask or think"), and we have three children and live in this neighborhood. *Snip.* His job is taking up more and more of his time. *Snip.* I might have to face my doubts and fears about adoption. *Snip.* All my pent-up anger and despising (like Esau) what God *has* blessed me with isn't getting me anywhere. *Snip. Snip. Snip.* The pruning was a graphic and healing demonstration of what God was doing in my life.

As the gardener of my little plot, I knew what I was doing. It would be absurd for the roses to tell me what to do or what they wanted. With every snip of my shears I was making sure they were stronger and healthier. The analogy became painfully obvious to me. Although I still couldn't see the purpose or results of what God was doing in my life, I knew that summer was coming, eventually. This season of pruning was preparation for another season soon to come. I'm not there yet—things are still tough—but this promise gave me hope. And hope is what Jesus is all about.

Growing Points

1. ~ Read John 15:1–8. What does Jesus say is the purpose of pruning? What hard time in your life felt as if you were being pruned?

2. ~ What sinful attitudes or stubborn traits do you think God was pruning? What emotions did you feel (anger, sorrow, depression, fear)?

3. ~ What "fruit" has come as a result of that pruning time?

4. ~ If you could prune an attitude out of your life, what would it be?

Oleander

I don't know why my mother thought the oleander plant was so special. Maybe because it grew down in Texas, where her mother was from and where my mother spent many vacations with her relatives as a child. Maybe because Wisconsin, where we lived, had such brutal winters that nobody could grow it. Or maybe because my mother's relatives had decorated birthday cakes with its pink and white blossoms (which you should never do—they're poisonous). Whatever the reason, my mother had an oleander plant that she pampered like an infant in intensive care.

The oleander had a special position in our glassed-in porch. Each June my mother would cajole my father into dragging the six-foot-tall plant and its heavy clay pot outside to thrive in our warm, humid Wisconsin summers. In the winter, she would pull it into the main house because sometimes the porch windows couldn't keep out the forty-below wind-chill factor. When the oleander bloomed, she wanted everyone to come see the small pink blossoms. Because she talked to it, pampered it, and babied it incessantly, I always thought that the oleander plant was some rare, hard-to-find specimen of the plant world.

When I moved to California from Wisconsin, I gained a new perspective about the preciousness of oleanders. Oleander plants were *everywhere*. They were about as precious as crabgrass. Schools, businesses,
homes—everyone had oleanders casually thrown into their landscaping
plans. Some had pink flowers, some white, others a delightful salmon
color. They were even used as plantings along the expressway median
strips. Stray bottles, trash, and the occasional car were thrown at these
hardy shrubs along the freeways. It is just another shrub like a yew or a
juniper, nothing special. I observed that our neighbors ruthlessly
whacked their oleanders back to three feet tall every year, and the plants
bounced right back to seven feet by the end of the summer. I now chuckle when I think back to how my mother cooed over and babied that oleander plant in our glassed-in porch.

I thought about my new perspective on the oleander recently when I heard an appeal on the radio. The
Bible League was talking about the need to supply
Bibles to China. (Despite what the secular media might
lead us to believe, Christians in China are undergoing
tremendous persecution for their faith. It didn't end
with Mao.) Even though Christians in China are losing
their jobs, being thrown in jail, and even being tortured for their faith, they do not want action. They
do not want you to write our president. They
do not want Amnesty International or the Unit-

ed Nations to drum up support. They do not want economic sanctions against the government. All they want, all they value, all they request from us are Bibles. To them the Bible is a rare and precious thing. From their perspective, it is more valuable than any other thing you could give them. More valuable than money, publicity, rights, or food. To them, the Word of God *is* food. Food for living. Food for freedom.

The Bible talks about this fact many times. "Trouble and anguish have come upon me; Yet Thy commandments are my delight" (Psalm 119:143 NASB). In the book of Matthew, Jesus had the Chinese believer's perspective when He responded to Satan's temptation of a meal while He was fasting: "It is written, 'Man shall not live on bread alone, but on every word that proceeds out of the mouth of God'" (4:4).

I don't know about you, but if I were being persecuted for my faith, if I lost my job for being a Christian, if my rights as an American citizen were being violated, requesting a Bible would not be the first thing I would think of. I would want someone to take legal action. I would want some radio program to let everyone know about how my and others' rights were being trampled. I would want change in my circumstances, not a Bible.

So then, I conclude, it's obvious that my perspective is skewed. I don't realize the power this one book has.

What is it about this book that makes it so powerful? Why do people have to smuggle it into some countries? If we read the biographies of people who have smuggled God's Word into countries in Eastern Europe, China, or the Middle East, we hear amazing stories. When one person gets his hands on a Bible, others painstakingly copy chapters and books by hand to memorize. Here in the West, we occasionally memorize verses that we feel might benefit us; they memorize *chapters*. It's a matter of survival for them.

John, a pastor in China, says, "There is a great revival here—it is easy to lead people to Christ. Yes, it is dangerous—31 of our leaders were arrested recently—but it makes us strong." Rachel, an evangelist, says, "There is a village where I work where only the leader has a Bible. It is passed around and shared and copied. We do not have enough Bibles." And there is Joshua, who recently spent more than two years in a hard labor camp for the crime of transporting Bibles. And yet, he wants more Bibles. "It is our bread, our life."[1]

In our home we have more Bibles than we need. I decided to take a tally and here's what I found: the Revised Standard Version, the Living Bible, the Message, the King James Version, the New King James Version (two copies), the New American Standard Version (two copies), the New International Version, the Serendipity Bible, the Amplified Bible, and the One Year Bible. That's twelve. One to suit whatever mood I'm in. A slim one for travel, a few study versions with lots of cross-references, and one version to help me slog through reading the entire Bible in a year. When I'm working on a Bible study, I have two or more versions lying

---

[1] Contact the Bible League at 800-334-7017 or *www.BibleLeague.org*. You can find out more about the persecuted church (and how you can help) at *www.persecution.com*.

around on the floor that I have to kick aside to get across the room. I wonder which one I'd want if I was in a jail cell for my faith. What version would suit my mood then? What would be my perspective on what was precious or important in my life?

My husband and I went to a Christmas party recently. We were overworked, overtired, and stressed about the unfinished Christmas shopping we had yet to do. We met a man there who didn't have a jaded view of the holiday season. He had a totally different perspective. He told us, "Last year, my trim, athletic wife had a heart attack at 43. She lay in a coma for two weeks. The doctors didn't have any answers or hope. Now she's healthy and back to normal. *Every day* is Christmas to us."

I enjoy many things as common in my life that I know other people would treasure: great health, a car to drive, a bike to ride, time to exercise, people to buy Christmas presents for, money to buy Christmas presents with, "problems" that are opportunities, food that's so plentiful that I have to diet occasionally, the freedom to worship, and the availability of God's Word. Now when I see the common oleander all over California, I think about the many things we have in abundance here in the Western world that are considered precious and valuable elsewhere. It's all a matter of perspective.

Growing Points

1. ≈ What would be the first three things you would want if you were imprisoned?

2. ≈ Have you ever had your rights trampled on? How did you feel? What did you do?

3. ≈ What things do you have that are common to you that most people in the world don't have?

4. ≈ What things do you get to do frequently that you most appreciate?

5. What blessings (health, wealth, talents) could you share with others who lack them?

Bullies

"I never met a man I didn't like," said Will Rogers. I don't feel that way about some plants. Some are bullies and thugs in the garden, and I think it's only fair to warn you about them.

One year I decided to have a primary color theme garden in the front yard. I had blue ground-cover morning glories, yellow daisies, and red gladiolas. It was garish and awful. The gladiolas needed staking, and I didn't have the time, so the afternoon winds whipped them around until they were hanging sloppily every which way. I pulled out everything but the blue morning glories.

Now lovely, cream-colored French Lace roses and pink snap dragons grace the front yard. Soothing, beautiful colors. However, even though I planted the primary color garden seven years ago, today I am still pulling out mini gladiolas that keep springing up. Each bulb begets tons of tiny baby bulbs. So when I pull up the main gladiola bulb, all the tiny bulbs that are attached fall off and scatter. Every year I think I've finally pulled out the last of them, but every year more come up. Now when I think of gladiolas, I shudder.

My garden catalog said yarrow would grow in any soil. That was an understatement. What it should have said was "This plant will spread and take over your garden. It will grow where you don't want it to. It will be nearly impossible to rip out. Year after year it will keep coming back, despite your best efforts."

I was talking about plants one day with an old friend. Her landscape designer had redone her garden, and she was listing the plants for me. When she got to yarrow, she stopped and said, "What is it with that *yarrow* stuff?" We both burst out laughing. For both of us, it was the invasive monster plant that we would never plant again.

I feel the same way about *Monarda*, or bee balm. I was so tempted by all the catalog and plant descriptions: "Attracts hummingbirds and butterflies." It sounded like the perfect, beneficial insect plant to have, and it came in purple and ruby red. It was pretty; it did attract pollinating bees, butterflies, and hummingbirds to my garden. Unfortunately, it had designs on the rest of my garden. I would hack it back and rip some out, only to see a huge patch stealthily spread from a four-inch transplant I had left behind. Suddenly the patch was up to a foot in diameter. I nearly dislocated my back trying to pull out that sneaky, well-rooted patch of *Monarda*. Never again, I vowed.

Mint is another plant, an herb, to be specific, that is renowned for gobbling up garden space. I like mint in my iced tea but not in my garden. I never have grown it, but my neighbor has, so consequently, I have it too. Despite the new redwood fence between our properties, her mint has crept underneath and raced along on my side of the fence. Monthly I rip out an area about seven feet by five feet. It's just amazing how fast and furious it spreads. My advice: Grow mint in a pot, not in your garden.

English ivy *(Hedera helix)* is very charming. I love quaint topiaries covered in its three-point leaves. However, it's also invasive. It can take over trees and smother native plants. I stupidly left a topiary pot on top of an empty area in the garden for two years. When I finally came back to it, it had rooted and spread like a flu bug. It was nearly unstoppable and extremely difficult to pull out.

Then there are the regular, everyday weeds—dandelions, crabgrass, and the like. I'm learning to just stop and yank them out at the first sign of them. Otherwise, they send down miles of tough roots, and you'll be sorry a week later when you're trying to pull them out.

According to scientists at the U.S. Department of Agriculture, invasive plants take over areas equaling twice the size of Delaware and require the use of eight billion dollars worth of pesticides. I wasn't surprised when I learned that my Japanese honeysuckle *(Lonicera japonicus)* is considered invasive by the Native Plant Conservation Initiative.[1] Fortunately, twice a year I go after that honeysuckle with my big hedge shears. I whack it back ruthlessly. Otherwise it would take over the neighborhood and maybe the state.

---

[1] For more information on invasive plants, visit *www.nps.gov/plants*.

There's another kind of bully we need to be ruthless with. You might think it's the legalistic, dour Christians at our churches who try to impose their rules on everyone. You might think it's the person who intimidates you and leaves you tongue-tied and fuming every time you meet. But, no, this bully is closer to the heart. This bully is your own self-condemning attitude. Her name is *Should*.

You can tell if Ms. Should is whispering in your ear if you hear yourself think or say, *I should put in extra time at the church. I should be the room mother at school. I should join this organization, they need me. I should do more, more, more.* Those *should* thoughts leave us feeling as if we aren't good enough, we don't have enough, and we aren't doing enough.

I laugh when I listen to Garrison Keillor's radio show, *A Prairie Home Companion*, on National Public Radio. Since I was born in the Midwest and am of Scandinavian descent, I relate to his sense of humor as he tells tales about the people of Lake Wobegon. When he talks about the church as *Our Lady of Perpetual Responsibility*, I chuckle with understanding. Guilt and *should* are familiar feelings that I try hard to shake.

When Tom and I were receiving premarital counseling, the therapist told a story about a woman who had a sign in her room that read, "Today, I will not *should* on myself." God doesn't *should* on us either. While we're thinking we should pray more, read more, give more, reach out more, be more involved, or volunteer more, He's thinking, *Be still and know that I am God.*

In Matthew 11:28, Jesus talks about desiring for us rest from the *shoulds* of life. "Come to me, all you who are weary and burdened, and I will give you rest."

How many items on our *should* list are generated from outside influ-ences? How many are from feelings of guilt instead of from what God has put on your heart? Don't let this *should* bully overburden you. Today, do not *should* on yourself.

Growing Points

1. ✒ What bullies do you have in your garden?

2. ✒ What bullies have you had in your life?

3. ✒ What is your *should* bully telling you to do today?

4. ✒ How does Matthew 11:28–30 say you can quiet *Should's* voice?

Breaking the Rules

❧

When I first got into gardening, I quickly learned that certain rules should be followed. Usually I discovered this through trial and error. The festive poinsettia plant I put on the doorstep at Christmas time shriveled and died at the slightest bit of frost (it's a native of Mexico). The house-plant I watered every day turned yellow and died (too much water).

A cursory glance through gardening catalogs and instructional books explains what conditions plants prefer. Some plants prefer sun, while some grow in shade. Some will thrive in your climate zone, while other plants won't. Some plants like lots of water, but other plants prefer drier conditions.

After reading the informative, instructional gardening materials, I moved onto books where gardeners talk about the *joy* of gardening. These were instructional as well, but more enjoyable—and sometimes hysteri-cal—to read. On every road trip my husband would find my nose buried in titles such as *People with Dirty Hands* by Robin Chotzinoff, *Slug Tossing* by Meg DesCamp, and *Full Bloom* by Rayford Reddell. Through these types of books I realized the old rules I had memorized about growing some plants weren't necessarily so.

Take, for instance, the rules about roses. Rayford Reddell writes,

> "Roses must have at least six hours of direct sunlight every day. Never plant rosebushes where you would plant ferns." For the first twenty years I grew roses, I sounded like a broken record, and grew increasingly impatient with people who asked which roses like growing in shade. "No roses like shade," I snapped back. "Plant azaleas and rhododendron." I was wrong.[1]

I had assumed from all of my reading that my roses would curl up and die if they didn't get their six hours of sunlight a day. Here was a guy saying the rules could be broken, within limits. He notes that even though a hybrid tea rose won't grow in shade, several kinds of roses *will*. I found this out for myself when I planted a lovely hybrid musk rose called Ballerina in a semishady spot near our front door. It has bloomed profusely with its cheerful, dainty, pink-and-white blossoms for four years. It receives mostly light shade and is obviously very happy.

It felt liberating and exciting to move beyond the stringent rules I had always accepted about gardening. It broadened my horizons; it freed me up.

---

[1] Rayford Reddell, *Full Bloom* (New York: Harmony Books, 1996).

Regarding tomato seeds or seedlings, all the gardening catalogs say, "Plant after the last frost date." Well, I don't have much patience, and I'm also ridiculously competitive. I want to have tomatoes before anyone else does. So I found a product that will allow my tomato plants to be happy, even if there's a heavy frost—or snow. They are little teepees of water that surround the plant with warmth stored from the sun. Pinetree Garden Seeds catalog[2] sells them under the name "Wall O Water." They work fabulously. And I'm delighted that I can break the rules and still come out ahead.

I now hardly pay any attention to the rules about correct spacing between plants. Usually, when you buy new plants from your local nursery or order them from a catalog, they say something like, "Allow twelve inches between plantings." That's great if you want that sparse, needs-to-grow-in-look for a year or two. If I go through the trouble of planning a garden, buying the materials, digging, and sweating, I want results. I don't want to wait a year or two for it to look lush and billowing with flowers. Dolly Parton was right when she said, "Less is not more, *more* is more!" (By the way, she has a fabulous rose named after her that I grow. It's huge, brazen red, and has a luscious scent.) So I break the rules. I crowd my plants. I can always thin them out later once they've grown in. My neighbors, in-laws, and friends think I'm so thoughtful, they are always getting free plants. I don't tell them they are a result of overplanting.

---

[2] Pinetree Garden Seeds, New Gloucester, Maine (207-926-3400 or *www.superseeds.com*).

I break the spacing rule with bulbs too. I plant bulbs (lilies, tulips, and daffodils) underneath perennials so that after they have finished blooming in the early spring, the perennials then rise up and camouflage their dying foliage. Bulbs need to be planted deep, so it works fine to do that underneath a surface-level perennial. When I plant bulbs in a container, they are side by side, squished in. That's the way they do it in the florists' shops when you buy tulips in bloom. How ugly would they look if they had followed the standard advice, "Plant tulip bulbs six inches apart"? You'd have one tulip per pot. Not attractive. Sometimes it's better to break the rules.

When some people come to faith in Christ, they break the customary rules as well. While I was in college, the *Four Spiritual Laws* pamphlet by Campus Crusade for Christ was ubiquitous. That's a good thing, because one of their similar publications, *The Spirit Filled Life*, was instrumental in moving me from religion to relationship with Jesus Christ. But I have to admit, I thought the approach was painfully corny. So much so that my pride got the best of me, and I declined to pray and receive Christ right there in front of my friend. I don't know if it was so much that, to me, praying in public was akin to bathing in public, or if it was that my pride

didn't want to admit that this little booklet held the key to what I was missing. It was probably a little bit of both. To this day, despite others hand-
ing out these tracts with tremendous soul-winning success, I can't do it.
That sort of approach didn't appeal to me then and doesn't now. And I
know that if my friends are like me (and they are), they wouldn't like it
either.

That's why stories of conversions like author Anne Lamott's leave
me chuckling and secretly delighted. Some people will swear that you
need to go forward to the altar during a service to make your decision for
Christ known, or for it to be a bona fide conversion experience. Others
think you only need to raise your hand "with every head bowed and every
eye closed." Anne Lamott's story shows that there is no right way, formula, or rule for coming into the kingdom. Anne writes,

> I became aware of someone with me, hunkered down in
> the corner.... The feeling was so strong that I actually turned
> on the light for a moment to make sure no one was there....
> But after a while, in the dark again, I knew beyond any doubt
> that it was Jesus. I felt him as surely as I feel my dog lying
> nearby as I write this. And I was appalled. I thought about my
> life and my brilliant hilarious progressive friends, I thought
> about what everyone would think of me if I became a Christ-
> ian.... I turned to the wall and said out loud, "I would rather
> die."
>
> And one week later, when I went back to church, I was so

hungover that I couldn't stand up for the songs.... I began to cry and left before the benediction, and I raced home...and I opened the door to my houseboat, and I stood there a minute, and then I hung my head and said, "... I quit." I took a long deep breath and said out loud, "All right. You can come in."

So this was my beautiful moment of conversion.[3]

That's not exactly the kind of conversion you hear about in a glowing testimony at a revival crusade, is it? People like Anne turn the rules upside down. Which, when you think about it, is exactly what Jesus did during His ministry on earth. The Pharisees were shocked that he would heal on the Sabbath. They didn't like Jesus breaking the rules. Anne's conversion account is raw, it's honest, and it's true. I think if we are honest with ourselves, those issues that made her waver are things that we all struggle with. We all want to be thought of as witty and brilliant.

Another breaking-the-rules story that makes me chuckle is one that speaker Dick Foth tells. He was working in Washington, D.C., among the power brokers and captains of politics. At one prayer breakfast, he offered to pray with a pretty tough character. The man said to him, "Okay, but I have two rules. I don't hold hands with guys and I won't close my eyes." Dick said that was fine, he didn't have to hold his hands, and he could keep his eyes open if he wanted to. Then the tough guy began to

---

3 Anne Lamott, *Traveling Mercies* (New York: Pantheon Books, 1999).

pray. He said, "God, (sigh), well, I know you've been trying like hell to get to me..." Not quite poetic prose, was it? But it was straight from the heart, to the point, and honest. I think God would rather have us raw and honest and without all the flowery words than to be disingenuous with Him.

I have a friend who is involved with a group that believes unless you are baptized in *their* church and follow *their* rules and doctrine, you are going to hell. They believe that they have the correct prescription for salvation. Follow their steps, their rules, and you are in. That's another reason I love Jesus. He kept showing us that the point was the *person* himself, not the method. We love to find rules and make sure everyone adheres to them. We get nervous if someone is comfortable being out of step with our methods.

The thief on the cross didn't have the *Four Spiritual Laws* pamphlet. He couldn't walk down the aisle at a crusade. He couldn't get into a confession booth. All he had was the desperate desire and plea of a dying man—"Remember me!" That the thief recognized Jesus' authority and divinity was enough for Jesus. Jesus answered him, "Today you will be with me in paradise." *Today*, not "after you've repented and shown me you mean it." Not "if you are baptized in this particular method" or "after you complete a class and join a church." Jesus said immediately, "Today

you will be with me in paradise." There's no record that the thief even *repented*, is there? That breaks some rules. I have to leave this conundrum with Jesus and rest in the fact that He knew the man's heart. Would that I could leave my own snap judgment of others' salvation to Jesus more often, instead of consigning them into my presumed categories.

To get the most bloom out of my garden, I have to break some rules. Maybe for God to display His glory through me, I have to allow Him to break my rules and suppositions about the way He works.

Growing Points

1. ✒ What were you taught while growing up about the proper way to approach God?

2. ✒ Do you ever pray in your car? At the kitchen sink? Where are some other places people pray?

3. ✒ Who do you know or who have you read about who has had an unusual experience in his or her Christian faith?

4 ✒ What expectations or rules do you have about how God will work through you to reach others?

High Maintenance

❧

"I'm a high-maintenance sleeper," she said with a smile. We were at a women's conference, and my new friend and roommate made this proclamation about herself as she set out her nighttime accoutrements—eight in total. Next to her bed she placed an alarm clock, earplugs, eye shade, pain pills, nose spray, mouth retainer, books, and water. Although I'm familiar with women who call themselves high maintenance (facials, pedicures/manicures, weekly salon appointments, etc.), I had never met a "high-maintenance sleeper" before. She was a bit quirky, but I understood why. Years ago she was in a car accident and suffered severe whiplash. She hadn't received physical therapy or help for her condition in the crucial early stages, and now pain was her constant companion. Every day and all night, her shoulders and neck throb with unrelenting fierceness. Doing simple things like emptying a dishwasher or turning her head are painful challenges. Despite this hardship, she's a fascinating conversationalist and budding theologian. I was excited to spend time with her, pondering the perplexities of the Scriptures.

I used to be a high-maintenance morning person. Before I found out my thyroid was too slow, mornings were almost a battleground between my husband and me. He's the type who bounds out of bed, full of vim and vigor, and expects all those around him to have the same wonder and joy for life. He even whistled. Once. (I really related to Proverbs 27:14, "If a man loudly blesses his neighbor early in the morning, it will be taken as a curse.") He soon learned that even though I am sitting up in bed, that doesn't mean I'm fully awake, and conversation is out of the question. My blood felt like syrup in my veins. My jaw seemed to be frozen in place. I always felt like I needed three more hours of sleep, and I was irritated that he was so well rested. He learned the hard way that he shouldn't attempt to talk to me until I had coffee and breakfast.

It was hard on him at times. He was so happy, innocent, and full of energy, and I was like the TV character Maude on steroids. It took a while, but he accommodated me. I like to think I was worth it, because later on in the day I metamorphized into a happy-go-lucky, brilliant version of June Cleaver. It must have been worth it, because he's still here, loving the quirky me.

High maintenance is only a problem if you don't value the object of your affection and think the end result is worth it. Ask a new car owner if spending hours waxing his car is too high maintenance, and he'll probably tell you it's a privilege.

Some odd, uninformed people out there think roses are too high maintenance. I love roses. I am sort of obsessed by them and have about forty varieties on our property. But as much as I love them, they are more work than most plants. I try to downplay this to people interested in growing roses because I want them to experience the pleasure of filling their homes with their own gorgeous roses. But I'm convinced roses are worth any high maintenance they might require. Yes, you do have to watch out for black spot, powdery mildew, aphids, and Japanese beetles, but thousands of gardeners around the world must think they're worth it because roses are called the queen of flowers. You don't hear that about trouble-free cacti, do you? Of course not. That's because roses—if you grow the right variety—are unbeatable for their beauty, masses of color, heavy perfume, and romantic appeal. They may be high maintenance, but they're also high value.

Some people think that dahlias are too high maintenance to grow. They whine, "Oh, you have to dig out the tubers every fall." To me, that little half-hour sacrifice of digging out the tubers (so they don't die in a hard freeze) is a small price to pay for the dahlia's unbeatable blooming power in any color imaginable. Toward the end of the summer, when everything else is looking bedraggled and spent, the dahlia is pumping out masses of flowers as if it's the first of June. They last all summer long and into the fall; they last at least a week in a vase. What's so high maintenance about that? I call that high value.

Oriental lilies require extra care in my garden. Because of the occasional critter in my yard, I plant the bulbs in gopher- and mole-proof cages. I have to bait for snails and slugs (they consider my lilies a delicacy). I have to spray for the moisture-sucking thrip insect. And sometimes, when lilies grow tall, I have to stake them so they don't fall over. But to smell an Oriental lily is to understand what the Victorians meant by the word *swoon*. One blossom can perfume an entire room. When I walk through the lobby of a fancy hotel in New York City or Hawaii, I always see bold, fragrant Oriental lilies in huge vases. They are opulent, exotic, and gorgeous. They are hideously expensive to buy per stem, so I get a special delight in growing them in my humble garden. I don't think about the maintenance. I think about the value and the pleasure.

I wonder sometimes if I'm a high-maintenance believer for God. Does He have to baby and pamper me, propping me up against the slightest wind of adversity? Do I need constant fertilizing from others, or can I feed myself from His Word? Is He getting high value in return? Am I using the gifts and talents He gave me to help others? Am I a fragrance of Christ to others? Am I willing to be uprooted and planted wherever and whenever He chooses? Or pruned and harvested for His purposes?

I would like to think that I am like my beloved lilies, intensely fragrant and lovely to look at but with the hardiness of a weed. No special care needed; He can depend on me to thrive. But the truth is, sometimes I *am* high maintenance. When I see someone who could benefit from my time or even just my prayers, I sometimes sink into my comfort zone and mutter, "Send someone else, Lord." When I'm struggling with decisions I sometimes want an *extra* sign from God of what to do, instead of acting responsibly on the truth I already know from His Word. How can we transform our natural tendency to be high-maintenance Christians into believers who return to Him high value for what He has invested in us? What does God consider as "high value"?

Paradoxically, high value isn't about anything we can do or achieve; it's about *being*. This is a little too Zen for most of us with a can-do attitude. We like to reach goals, get awards, and receive recognition for our efforts. But Jesus teaches us that the secret is in just hanging out in the right place, with the right focus. He describes for us where that place is in the Gospel of John: "Remain in me, and I will remain in you. No branch can bear fruit by itself; it must remain in the vine. Neither can you bear fruit unless you remain in me. I am the vine; you are the branches. If a man remains in me and I in him, he will bear much fruit; apart from me you can do nothing.... This is to my Father's glory, that you bear much fruit" (15:4–5,8). In other words, am I falling in love with Jesus? Is that my daily focus? Everything else will flow out of that.

This spring, I'm going to cut some branches off my apple tree so I can enjoy the blossoms indoors. Even though I might put fertilizer in the water, give the branches plenty of light, and encourage them as much as possible, they are not going to produce apples after they bloom. They have been separated from the apple tree. The branches are not the reason they are laden with apples every fall; it's what the branches are attached to, the tree. The tree feeds it nutrients down through the branches and allows them to produce fruit. All the branches have to do is remain on the tree. Just being there, in the right place, causes the fruit to develop on the branches. All the branches don't individually worry about how much fruit they will produce. They are not busily trying to catch the raindrops that fall; they just need to remain attached to the tree and it will happen.

So too with us. All of our efforts to do the right thing—serve on this or that committee, work work work at our high-maintenance religion—won't get us any closer to God. It won't make Him love us any more. The super-busy Christian do-er is not what Jesus said is "to his Father's glory." But remaining in Him, just being one with Him, is how we produce fruit. That's not a high-maintenance religion but a relationship that's of high value to God.

Growing Points

I. ∞ Do you know anyone who is high maintenance?

2. ∞ In what ways does that attitude bother or inconvenience you?

3. ∞ In what areas are you high maintenance?

4. ∞ What specific steps can you take to "remain in the vine"?

My neighbors must think I'm odd, scurrying around in the dark. Whenever I leave on a trip I don't spend much time packing, but I do spend a lot of time getting the garden ready. I'm leaving early tomorrow morning, and instead of packing or writing instructions for the house-sitters, I've spent the last several hours—way past when the sun went down—preparing the garden.

bugs

The roses looked like they needed some protection from the thrips that had been sucking the life out of them and preventing the buds from opening. So I spent a half hour spraying them. Then I had to look after the tomato seedlings that would probably die if they weren't watered every day. I worried that our friends who were house sitting might overlook them in watering, so I spent an hour potting them. The raspberry bushes that I moved (I did it later in the season than I should have) needed some extra care. I watered them along with the beans, basil, and peppers that are in the raised beds.

Since I'm going to be gone, I thought, *why leave all those roses on the bushes? Why not bring them into the house for bouquets for my friends to enjoy?* So then I spent an hour or so doing that. I moved the window boxes around (some get sun, some get shade) and watered them. I'm so predictable in this behavior that my husband bought me a head lamp, like miners use, so I could see in the dark.

The Boy Scout motto "Always be prepared" makes the difference between coming home to a bug-eaten, water-starved, disease-ridden garden and a well-prepared haven of welcome. I am starting to learn, through trial and error, the benefits of preparing ahead of time. Sometimes it's not a tool I need to be prepared for a task, but the conditions need to be prepared.

In our area we have what is called clay soil. ~~I think that's a euphemism.~~ It's more like cement. Or, if the area hasn't seen water in a month or so, I'd call it iron. Nothing—no spade, no shovel—will penetrate it. I once watched a 187-pound man (we won't mention names) jump on a shovel in an attempt to dig into the soil. He bounced off.

I thought, *Oh, that's easy, we'll just water.* The water ran right off. To get the soil softened so I could dig, I had to put a hose on it with water barely dribbling out for a couple of hours. Better yet was waiting for a long spring rain. Only after that could I turn over the soil and add compost to amend it. I couldn't just jump in and work in the garden; I had to carefully prepare the soil.

When I read accounts of people who accomplish great things for God, I see the same principle of preparation at work. I notice that godly people strive to prepare themselves for a life of loving God, serving Him, and sharing His love with others. Then they receive the highest accolade— not to be called "successful," which is fleeting, but rather "faithful." When Jesus told the parable about the talents entrusted to the slaves to invest, His loftiest praise was for the one who invested wisely. Jesus said, "Well done, good and faithful slave; you were faithful with a few things, I will put you in charge of many things, enter into the joy of your master" (Matthew 25:21 NASB).

A more recent example of being faithful, and one that made an enduring impression on me, was Hudson Taylor's life. Hudson Taylor often is referred to as the father of modern missions. He founded the China Inland Mission and reached thousands of Chinese for Christ in the nineteenth century. He had a new approach for missions in his day, one of which was to take strong steps of preparation to identify with the people of China. He adopted their style of dress and lived like they did.

Yes, Hudson Taylor felt called by God to go to China. Yes, he loved God with all his heart. But he knew that that wasn't enough to reach the souls in China; he needed to prepare himself.

"At once he began to prepare, as well as he could, for a life that would call for physical endurance. He took more exercise in the open air, exchanged his feather bed for a hard mattress and was watchful not to be self-indulgent at table."[1]

This remarkable man taught himself Chinese using a copy of the Gospel of Luke in Chinese and comparing verses with his English version. Through this method he learned the meaning of more than six hundred characters. To spend more of his money on others and less on himself, Taylor moved out of his comfortable lodgings and into a twelve-by-twelve room with rudimentary furniture in a plain cottage on the poor side of town. Step by step he emptied himself of "needs" and comforts to identify with those in lack, those to whom he would be ministering.

We readily understand our need for preparation for a job. We go to the right schools and get the right training so we can climb the ladder of success. We understand preparing for a race. We train and exercise discipline and our muscles. But there is a destination that I don't think we give much thought to preparing for: our eventual home, heaven.

The only thing we can take to heaven is our character. Not our volunteer hours, not our church attendance, not our good deeds, and certainly not our material stuff. We will be stripped of everything from this life that we hold so dear when we stand before the entrance. If we know Christ personally, He has paid our entrance fee, but what we offer to God

---

[1] Dr. and Mrs. Howard Taylor, *Hudson Taylor's Spiritual Secret* (Chicago: Moody Press, 1981), 23.

is our character. (I don't want to lament with Cardinal Wolsey, "Would that I had served my God the way I have watched my waistline!"[2])

So how can we prepare for heaven? How is character developed? I've heard that character is molded by the secret daily choices that nobody sees. But I don't agree. That sounds very works-oriented and turns into a do-it-yourself project in which, if you make enough consistent "good" choices, you become a good person. I believe the inner work on the heart, the development of character, is accomplished by letting your relationship with Jesus influence your choices. Turning the daily events of your life over to Him so His character becomes yours. This is a relationship-oriented process versus a performance-oriented process. Right choices, big ones and small ones, flow out of our relationship with Jesus Christ. Character is *revealed* by our daily choices. Character is shaped by this daily, communicative process of surrendering our will to His will.

While the idea that character develops through our relationship with God rather than our performance might sound too cushy, it's actually anything but cushy. It takes place in the crucible of suffering. We see this principle in Paul's letter to the Romans: "But we also rejoice in our sufferings, because we know that suffering produces perseverance; perseverance, character; and character, hope" (5:3–4). A godly character grows through right responses and perseverance in tough circumstances. What is our response when things don't go our way? Do we rage at the unfairness? Do we pout? Give up? Strike back in anger? Try to seize control?

---

[2] Brennan Manning, *Abba's Child* (Colorado Springs: NavPress, 1994), 33.

Or do we follow the advice of Paul in his letter to the Philippians: "Rejoice in the Lord always; again I will say, rejoice! Let your forbearing spirit be known to all men....Be anxious for nothing....Practice these things; and the God of peace shall be with you" (4:4–6, 9 NASB).

Life on earth is prep school for another life to come. We all, at one time or another, will take the prerequisite course of suffering. It is not an easy course. Sometimes it can take years to graduate. If you read the chapter 12 on pruning, you know that I certainly didn't have a great response when I first started my course. But our God is a God of grace, and we can be confident "that he who began a good work in you will carry it on to completion until the day of Christ Jesus" (Philippians 1:6). As long as we keep turning to Him, responding to the tough situations in life with choices of trust and faithfulness, we will enter heaven fully prepared with a gift for the One who suffered for us. We won't be embarrassed that we didn't do anything with the gifts and talents He entrusted to us. We will be able to hear with joy, "Well done, good and faithful servant."

One of America's favorite writers, Erma Bombeck, wrote the following, which I've taped above my computer.

I always had a dream that when I am asked to give an accounting of my life to a higher court, it will go like this: "So, empty your pockets. What have you got left of your life? Any dreams that were unfulfilled? Any unused talent that we gave you when you were born that you still have left? Any unsaid compliments or bits of love that you haven't spread around?"

And I will answer, "I've nothing to return. I spent everything you gave me. I'm as naked as the day I was born."[3]

---

3 Erma Bombeck, *Forever Erma* (Kansas City: Andrews and McMeel, 1996), xiii.

Growing Points

1. ❧ What goals did you reach in life (school, athletics, awards) that you invested time preparing for? How did you feel about that preparation time?

2. ❧ Read Luke 10:38–42. Which woman can you relate to? Which woman did Jesus think had spent her time wisely?

3. ❧ What would you change in your daily life to prepare for eternity in heaven?

4. ❧ What character traits would you like to take with you when you meet your Savior face to face?

The Desert

✺

Thanks to Hollywood, many of us are afraid of the desert. It conjures up images of vultures circling a hapless victim about to die. Plants with sharp, don't-touch-me spines survive in the desert. The sun is fierce, and the nights are frigid. Gardeners receive the words *heat wave* and *drought* with dread. We marshal forces to stave off any desertlike conditions from occurring in our gardens. Even people who live in desert areas try to deny it by pouring gallons of water into their lush, England-inspired lawns and flower beds.

I, too, wanted to avoid the desert, but we were in Phoenix on a business trip for my husband, and the only garden around was the Desert Botanical Garden of Phoenix. I thought it was kind of ironic. I was feeling very much like a desert myself—dried up and barren. My writing reservoir of ideas seemed to have run dry, and I felt as if my womb was going to be forever barren as well. After four years of pursuing every fertility treatment known to science, the cliché *life isn't fair* took on new poignancy for me.

"Why don't you visit that Desert Botanical Garden we read about?" Tom suggested. Since I love to visit gardens when I travel, he figured this would get my mind on other things for a while. "There's no *life* in the desert! Why on earth would I want to see dried-up ground and prickly cacti?" I asked him. "It sounds totally boring to me." But I soon found out that hanging around the pool all day was boring, so I set off to find this place.

Walking through the gates, the first thing I saw were cacti, of course. But instead of murmuring *How typical and boring* to myself, I was surprised. These weren't the stereotypical cacti of a western movie; there was incredible variety. There were Beaver Tail, Prickly Pear, Teddy Bear, and a purple octopus cactus *(Stenocereus alamosensis)*. There was a tremendous diversity of shapes and colors—anything but boring. I even became enamored with several specimens and took notes to look them up at my local nursery when I got home.

As I walked along the gravel paths, I noticed something else. Because of the intense heat, I moved much slower. I didn't rush around from plant to plant as I would have normally. And because I was moving at a slower pace, my awareness and sensitivity to my surroundings became heightened. I spied a small, shy desert tortoise ambling along the fenced-off section of wild flowers. Most people missed him, thinking he was a rock. But I got to watch his determined efforts to get a taste of the forbidden flora.

I also noticed a peacefulness. Just as the heat seemed to blanket the area, a heavy stillness and tranquillity covered the garden and me. Hearing a soft, fluttering sound, I lifted my head to the majestic saguaro cactus towering over me. Two cactus wrens were happily building a nest. Apparently, nobody had told them there was no life in the desert.

Walking around a bend in the path, I was surprised to see a cacophony of color. Some of the cacti had the most extraordinary blooms. Amidst the sharp thorns and despite the dry conditions, they had exploded in vibrant fuchsias, oranges, and yellows. Even the surrounding rocks were painted in a gorgeous palette of red and ochre. It seemed incongruous to have such color and beauty in a desert—a place associated with tough conditions and death.

I smiled to myself as I thought of my attitude earlier in the day, *Who wants to look at a bunch of prickly, uninviting cacti in an inhospitable setting?* Like many, I thought the desert symbolized death, personified by painter Georgia O'Keeffe's bleached skulls. I remembered the movies from my youth depicting people crawling across the barren desert landscape gasping, "Water! Water!" I hadn't welcomed the idea of going to the desert, just like the Israelites hadn't. "Why can't we go back to Egypt?" they whined. But good things come from the desert.

God uses the desert to shape our character and to strengthen us. Just as the potter's kiln strengthens and hardens the clay, so do desert times for us. In the desert, Moses and the Israelites had to rely on God. Even though God demonstrated His power by parting the Red Sea, His care and provision with the manna, His thoughtfulness with the alternative quail to eat, and His faithfulness with a pillar of fire at night and a cloud by day, the Israelites rebelled—they doubted. Although He never let them down and supplied their every need, they made a golden calf to worship instead. Consequently, only Joshua and Caleb of that first generation, because of their faithfulness in trusting God, were allowed to see the Promised Land. God said about Caleb, "He will see it, and I will give him and his descendants the land he set his feet on, because he followed the Lord wholeheartedly" (Deuteronomy 1:36).

This was no small thing. It's hard to trust God in the midst of suffering, when you don't know how the story is going to end. It's hard to have faith when all circumstances point toward a negative ending. But apparently, it's critically important to God that we believe His Word. It's important to Him that we depend upon Him in our desert times when we're stripped of our resources, that we trust and believe in what He said—no matter how barren the landscape looks. The desert reveals what sort of people we are.

John the Baptist spent the majority of his life in the desert (Luke 1:80)—a place devoid of the distractions and entertainments of this world. He depended on God for provision. This experience shaped him into a person who people noticed. Jesus said about him, "I tell you the truth: Among those born of women there has not risen anyone greater than John the Baptist" (Matthew 11:11).

Jesus spent time in the desert too. It was his place of testing, of maturing, of preparing for His earthly ministry. After forty days of prayer and fasting in the desert, He was able to face a full onslaught of Satan's biggest temptations.

For us to grow as people and as believers, we have to endure some time in the desert. In our desert times we have to trust God when we don't know the end of the story. The apostle Paul set a great example of this while he was imprisoned. He encouraged the Philippians: "Rejoice in the Lord always. I will say it again: Rejoice! Let your gentleness be evident to all. The Lord is near. Do not be anxious about anything" (Philippians 4:4–6). Paul had plenty of reasons to be anxious in his life. He had been stoned, shipwrecked, mocked, and imprisoned, yet he had confidence in the God who allowed those circumstances. We have to decide whether or not we're going to trust God in the middle of the story. We need to have faith when it doesn't look as if our story will end well. From our viewpoint, suffering challenges the glory of God. From God's viewpoint, it helps shape us into the person God intended us to be.

When I was walking through the Desert Botanical Garden, I realized how quickly my priorities would change if I were forced to live there for a week. My list of necessities for daily life would narrow down immediately to just food, shelter, and clothing. All the other blessings and comforts I enjoy are just that—comforts—not necessities. It's important to note when the Israelites were wandering in the desert, God provided for their every need. They were only miserable when they took their eyes off of what was provided and focused instead on the luxuries they missed.

For some of us, the greater miracle is not getting *out* of the desert, escaping the hard times, but remaining faithful and believing in God's goodness in the midst of it. We know God's promises tell us there is a good ending. But it's hard to believe that in the middle of the desert. Our toughest lesson is believing in God's goodness when we're challenged by betrayal, job loss, relationship failure, sickness, or heartache.

I often prayed to God, reminding Him of His pregnancy miracles with Sarah, Hannah, and Mary. To make me pregnant would be a small miracle for Him. He who could divide the Red Sea and cure the cripple could surely do this without batting an eye. And in my heart I heard His response to me, "You're right, Laurie, this would be a small, easy miracle for me to do. But the *greater* miracle would be to see your heart change. To see you still praise and love me even if you were never to have children."

I still don't know the end of my story. But I do know that my job is to keep praising Him in the midst of my desert times and to keep enjoying the life and blessings He has provided for me. As I strolled through Phoenix's Desert Botanical Garden, I couldn't miss the message this garden held for me.

Although my situation seemed barren, with no life stirring within me, I realized there *were* signs of life going on—just a different sort. I had been moving too fast, relentlessly chasing my goal, to notice the gifts in the desert time of my life.

I have a kind, sensitive husband who is my rock and faithfully stands by me. I have a good relationship with my family and a sense of peace that they will accept whatever I decide to do. I have the blessing of a quiet and tranquil home so I can write and listen for spiritual lessons. I have interesting and colorful friends who are a delight to spend time with and are quick to cheer me up. I have the gift of robust health; I daily bike, hike, or use the gym.

As I was heading out of the Desert Botanical Garden, I read this message on an engraved marker:

> The most significant lesson that desert dwellers can learn…is to regard themselves not as exiles from some better place, but as people at home in an environment to which life can be adjusted.[1]

Yes, there is life in the desert, and I was not only going to learn to adjust, but I was also going to go home and appreciate its gifts.

---

[1] Forest Shreve, *The Cactus and Its Home,* 1931.

Growing Points

1. When have you been through desert times in your life?

2. How did you feel about those times? How did you feel about God?

3. What did you learn that drew you closer to God or that you could pass on to others?

4. Read 2 Corinthians 6:3–10 and 11:23–31. What sort of desert experiences did Paul go through?

Last year was "The Year of the Mole" in my garden. Moles travel underground and heave up the dirt and sod as they go. They disturb plants and separate the roots from the soil. Consequently, plants die. The moles were *everywhere*. I tried everything to get rid of them. They were baffling. I've lived in the same house for seven years and never had them before. Why now? Why here?

Garden pests are a fact of life. Every garden, no matter how professional, famous, or fabulous, has to deal with pests. They come in a variety of shapes and sizes, and different ones appear in different seasons. I didn't get any answers to my whys, but I did get to work.

The first thing I tried was a vibrating spike device. The theory is that all you need to do is sink it into the ground and insert the batteries, and the vibration will scare the moles away. Instead, they seemed to think a party was going on with a great beat. They cruised around that spike like it was a maypole.

Next I tried a Mole-Be-Gone concoction. This was a formula of mostly castor oil that I bought through a catalog. It, too, was supposed to thwart their advances. All it accomplished was to kill two rosebushes because I had poured so much into the soil. (The company refused to reimburse me for my two favorite rosebushes.) Now I was angry and obsessed.

I started to behave like Bill Murray in the movie *Caddyshack*, in which he portrayed a disheveled golf-course groundskeeper obsessed with getting rid of a pesky gopher. I studied up on mole behavior and learned the best time to catch them. Unfortunately, I learned they travel mostly at night. Some nights I would slip out of bed in hopes of catching the moles as they moved about our lawn.

"Where are you going at this hour?" Tom would ask with sleepy-eyed bewilderment.

"Outside to catch those stupid moles!" I answered as I grabbed the flashlight and shovel. I crept around, waited silently in the dark, and stared at the lawn for what felt like hours for any signs of the earth moving. But I couldn't catch them in the act. All I caught was a frozen and stiff behind. I went to bed angrier than ever.

The next morning I called my sister. She lives twenty miles away in an area that's gopher heaven. I figured if she could keep the gophers away, she'd know what to do about my moles.

"What you need," she said with authority, "is my trapper."

"A trapper? You mean like a sort of Gopher Dundee?"

"Make fun if you want to, but he's the only thing I've tried that works."

Who was I to argue with a woman who successfully manages her own ten acres? I called her trapper.

He came and set up some metal traps around the yard. I had tried metal spring-loaded traps before, too, but his were different. He studied the mole trails and set the traps delicately right over and inside the main passageways. "I'll be back in about a week," he said.

I hoped that something (the something being death to a mole) would happen sooner than a week. The next afternoon, I heard the sweetest sound ever coming from my backyard. It wasn't the melodic sound of a songbird, and it wasn't the hum of bees pollinating flowers. It was the loud, metallic *snap!* of one of the traps snaring a mole. The sound of sweet victory. The sound of certain death.

Eventually, the trapper got rid of all the moles. And my garden appears to be free of them. But other pests still lurk out there, waiting for a chance to devour my plants.

I've had snails in abundance since day one of my gardening life. No matter what I do, they are an everpresent threat to the garden. I used to like snails—to eat them, I mean. But after a few years of stepping on them and feeling them squish through my toes and picking them off my plants by the thousands, I detest them. When I first moved to California I thought having snails in my garden was neat. I marveled, "My very own escargot!" But now the thought of eating them nauseates me. I constantly make the rounds in the garden with my plastic bag of salt. I drop the snails in the bag and the game's over. Other methods I also employ to keep them in check are snail bait (vegetable and pet safe, of course) and beer. Yes, like the magnet Fort Lauderdale is to college students, beer is to snails. They throw themselves with gusto into the beer and drown.

A pest that I'm on the lookout for every spring is the tiny aphid. Every spring aphids try to suck the life out of my rosebuds. You can tell your roses have aphids if the buds are slow to open and the petals look kind of crusty and leathery. Sometimes the stems will bend over, unable to support the weight of the bud. Do not despair; there is a simple solution. Organic insecticidal soap kills them and keeps them away (your local nursery will have some). You have to reapply it after a rain, but it's far better for your roses and the environment than the other more powerful and hazardous chemicals.

I'm not upset about aphids and snails like I was about the moles. Because I know these pests come every spring, just like daffodils and tulips, I expect them and am prepared for them. Unfortunately, other pests in my life catch me by surprise. These pests are in my spiritual life.

Sometimes it's a small pest, like an irritation or a bothersome situation. At certain times of the month I know that I will find Tom or other people unbelievably irritating. If I combine that with an overloaded schedule and too little sleep, I begin to erupt. I'll snap at people and say things I wish I hadn't. Then it's as if I've taken an overly powerful chemical like Agent Orange and wiped out my perceived attacker. My acidic comments kill relationships, and I end up regretting what I said and having to make amends.

For those small irritations—the woman who cut in front of you at the bank, the friend who gossiped about you, your spouse's bad attitude— you can apply our spiritual insecticidal soap, the Scriptures. God's Word kills off negative thoughts and prevents more from starting and festering. Philippians 4:8 says, "Whatever is true, whatever is noble, whatever is right, whatever is pure, whatever is lovely, whatever is admirable—if anything is excellent or praiseworthy—think about such things." Instead of focusing on what a jerk someone is, we can be transformed by the renewing of our minds (see Romans 12:2). We can think about the good and positive things. Maybe it's as basic as, "Well, I'm glad other people are patient with *me* when I act like that!"

Sometimes the small irritations are your own negative thoughts that buzz around your head like pesky gnats, thoughts like, *I'm no good. It'll never work out. If people could see who I really was inside, they wouldn't like me. I'll bet even God's not all that thrilled with me.* Those are the thoughts of the oppressor. Sure, they sound like me and they come from my brain, but only because I'm tuned into the enemy's channel. How do we inoculate and protect ourselves from being weakened, depressed, and overcome by his negative schemes? We clean it all out with insecticidal soap—God's Word. Scripture therapy. It means replacing the negative lies with the truth.

I used to resent this approach; I thought it was like brainwashing myself. But then I realized that the world is constantly filling my brain with its songs, billboards, magazine and newspaper articles, and ads. It's all around me all the time! These messages say I'm not good enough, I don't have enough, and I'm missing out. No wonder we're all run ragged trying to keep up.

Just as a plant needs to be fertilized and watered to remain healthy to withstand the onslaught of pest invasions, so we need to keep ourselves spiritually healthy to withstand the pest invasions in our lives. This is the path to peace. To me, the key to that Philippians verse on "think about such things" is what comes next. In the following verse, the apostle Paul says, "Whatever you have learned or received or heard from me, or seen in me—*put it into practice. And the God of peace will be with you*" (Philippians 4:9).

If you doubt the efficacy of this approach, look at what Jesus did. When tempted by Satan in the desert, Jesus used only one weapon, a weapon we can use just as easily. Every time Satan offered Him something, Jesus responded with the spoken Word of God. He quoted Scripture, God's truth, back to Satan. Matthew 4:1–11 shows us the devil's response. He would try a different tactic. Eventually, he gave up. The Word of God is powerful. Quote it back to your negative thoughts; quote it back to the enemy of your soul who is pestering you. Read it, memorize it, and ask the Holy Spirit to show you how to apply it to your daily life.

Sometimes a big pest, like sickness in the family, in-law problems, or financial setbacks descend on your life. Then it can feel like a bear stomping over your garden, ripping up and destroying everything in its path. We wonder, as I did when the moles attacked, *Why now? Why this?* but we don't always get any answers.

Parroting back Scripture in response to tragedy isn't a cure-all for the broken heart. In these situations all I can do is fall on my knees and beg for God's mercy. I read everything I can in the Bible about God's love for me and His sovereignty. The psalms help a lot here. I try to turn the situation over to the professional trapper, Jesus Christ. I ask Him to take control of everything. I ask for His will to be done. Sometimes I have to do all this hourly.

It's a fact of life that pests will always invade a garden and pests will infest our daily lives. Expect pests and prepare for them and you'll not only withstand the attack but also thrive in spite of it.

Growing Points

1. What are some pests in your life right now?

2. How are you currently dealing with them?

3. What might be a more effective way to control them and keep them from weakening you?

4. What are some unexpected pests that have shown up?

5. What are some pests that you regularly expect?

Tricks

❧

You'd think that after spending my formative years watching my award-winning mother and grandmother make glorious floral arrangements I would've learned a few tricks. Unfortunately, I think I had my nose in a book or was at the local pool while they were executing their floral genius. However, in the last few years I have begun to study in earnest the floral arrangement tricks gardeners employ both in the garden and inside the home.

When I was quite young, my mother and my grandmother were forever soaking brick-shaped Oasis® floral foam for their various arrangements. They would place it in the bottom of a container or bowl and stick flowers into it. I thought it was mainly to keep them watered. But now I know floral foam is the secret to professional-looking arrangements because it holds the flowers upright, in the exact position and angle you set them in. So no more plunking flowers into water and having them droop every which way into a haphazard "arrangement."

Typically, you don't use floral foam in a vase. A vase has high sides, which provide good support. Floral foam is more for nontraditional vessels for displaying flowers, such as shallow bowls, plastic-lined baskets, or any odd-shaped container with no visible means of support for the long stems of flowers.

The first time I used Oasis® floral foam was in an arrangement for a friend's party. I really didn't know what I was doing, but I figured I had enough flowers to create three arrangements if I had any trouble. I got a narrow basket because it was going on a narrow table where food was being served. I soaked the foam and plunked it down into the plastic interior. Then I taped it down, across the top and slightly over the sides of the basket. Next I began inserting the filler, which is typically greens or variegated foliage to form a backdrop. Just as trees create the background for a meadow of wild flowers, filler helps the stars—your flashy flowers—stand out.

After I had the back and sides pretty much filled in, I started putting in the stars. The roses, lilies, tulips, snapdragons, and breath of heaven all were inserted in sort of an arch shape (long on the sides and center). Then I stood back. I looked at it from various angles and noticed where I could still see some tape on the basket. I grabbed some more filler and baby's breath and plunked it in to cover up the visible tape and gaps in the arrangement. Voilà! I had a professional-looking arrangement people oohed and aahed over. I worried it looked a little too traditional and large, like a funeral arrangement for a casket, but everyone assured me it was fabulous. That's how easy working with floral foam is.

For vases, there are two tricks to get your flowers to stay exactly where you want them. But first I should mention the number one mistake people make when putting flowers into vases—they leave the stems too long. I always cut about a third to half the length off the bottom. Flowers that are too tall won't hold up well in a vase, no matter what tricks you use.

The first thing you need is a frog. No, not the kind that hops and croaks. In florist terms, a frog is a weighted round disk with spikes or a wire grid. This goes in the bottom of the vase. You press the flower stems into it and the "teeth" or the grid grabs the stems and holds them in position. The other trick is to tape the top of the vase. You can do this with green floral tape or clear, office-type tape. Just place strips of it across the mouth of the vase to make a grid and anchor the tape slightly over the sides. Now when you put the flowers in, they won't flop to one side; the grid holds them in place.

Getting cut flowers to last a long time involves other strategies. All cut flowers need sugar for nourishment and an acidic ingredient, such as aspirin or lemon-lime soda. This makes the water easier to drink. A tiny bit of bleach prevents bacterial growth. That's the basic formula for all flower arrangements.

Some plants, especially woody-stemmed flowers such as lilacs, forsythia, dogwood, and camellias, need a little stronger treatment. They should be split vertically up from the bottom so that more water can be drawn up. Only about an inch or two is needed. If the stem is very thick, smash the last few inches with a hammer until it is frayed. Lilacs, I have heard, last longer if you put them in wood alcohol for an hour and then into cold water and a cool place overnight.

I have also heard that if your roses look limp or the heads are starting to nod, submerge them (as if they were taking a bath) in a sink of cool water and cover the stems with a towel. I don't know about that approach, but I do have one that worked wonders for me. My sister got this tip from a woman who created arrangements for the British royal family and lectured at a course my sister took. It's amazing.

The day after I bought some roses, they looked as if they were in a coma. Every single head was drooping. I was distraught because I was supposed to make an arrangement for a friend's party. I looked at them and decided I had nothing to lose by trying the royal florist's approach. I got the water coming out of the kitchen faucet as hot as it would get, filled a pitcher with the hot water, and placed the roses in it. I was sure I was killing them, but my sister said it was supposed to revive them. It did! An hour later, they all stood upright, like soldiers at attention. Author Rayford Reddell says this process (called hardening) works even better if you mix the florist's preservative solution (those freebie packets of powder you get with arrangements) in with the hot water. The flowers absorb the preservative better when they are in hot water. Then after your roses have perked up, recut the stems *under* water.

Another strange and torturous trick to reviving flowers is sticking pins in your tulips. Tulip heads will droop quite quickly, but if you stick a straight pin just below the head of the flower and then pull it out, you will allow trapped air to escape. This increases the flow of water all the way up. However, you can avoid this trapped air problem with tulips and all your other flowers by recutting them under water. That allows them to immediately draw up water, not air. Some people also swear by putting a few copper pennies in the bottom of a vase of tulips to prevent drooping. But according to Frans Roozen, technical director of the International Flower Bulb Center in Hillegom, Holland, this isn't true. "Tulips are self-sufficient. Just add clean water, that's all," says Mr. Roozen.

Sometimes we want our favorite flowers to bloom indoors for a special event. If the season is over for that flower, a call to the local florist is in order. But if it's peonies you want, you don't need to call a florist. My sister and her husband have a summer place in our hometown of Madison, Wisconsin. One year, I was visiting there on my own, and she called me to ask how the garden was doing. She was heartsick that she was missing the peonies blooming. So we tried an experiment we had heard about.

I cut some peonies while they were still in the bud stage, before the flowers had opened but after the green sepals had separated slightly to barely reveal the color of the petals. I took them inside and wrapped each bud in plastic wrap. (Some people advocate wrapping all the stems and buds together in one wrap. I did each separately.) I set all of the stems with their wrapped buds into a vase of water, and put them in my sister's extra refrigerator. It's important that the flowers go into a refrigerator without any fruits or vegetables; the ethylene gas produced naturally by the food will wreck the flowers. Over a month later, my sister came into town and pulled the arrested stems out of the refrigerator and unwrapped them. They bloomed beautifully.

Moving from cut flowers to plants, there are some tricks you can employ outside. Roses respond like we do to a soak of Epsom salts—you can almost hear them saying "aaahhhhh." For your average rosebush, a half cup of Epsom salts is perfect. Just sprinkle it around the base and water it in well. Your roses will respond by aggressively sending out new shoots of growth. This is because Epsom salts contain magnesium sulfate—thereby supplying magnesium—a nutrient essential for plant growth. I do this about twice a year for my roses.

I'm a pack rat when it comes to seed packages. I hate to throw them away. And this makes sense, because some seeds are viable for several years. (Unfortunately, some aren't.) How can you tell? This is what I do with seeds I'm considering sowing. I test them by putting several between two sheets of paper towels. I dampen the paper towels and then slide the packet into a plastic sandwich bag, but I don't close it. I leave the bag in a warm, sunny window. If in a few days the seeds sprout, I know there's still some oomph left in them. If not, I throw them out.

Sometimes my faith feels as if all the oomph has drained out of it. I feel no enthusiasm for church, reading the Bible, or anything to do with any of it. Are there some tricks we can use to get our Christian life up and running again? Yes, there are. I've seen other people doing these things and I do them too.

If I'm shell-shocked by some event in life or I'm just too depressed or upset to face God about something, I'll spend a couple of days reading good Christian fiction or a Christian biography. This is sort of the back-door approach to softening my heart. I find afterward that I end up reflecting on the goodness and power of God. I marvel on how much the people in the books (fiction and nonfiction) went through and realize my problems are not such a big deal. I'm reenergized about the things of God.

Another thing I do is sing. I bought a hymnal a few years ago. It's wonderful to look up old favorites and sing them to myself when nobody's around (I'm a lousy singer). The words in those fourth and fifth stanzas that you don't remember or don't always get to sing in church are poetic and moving. If I'm not in the mood for old hymns, I put on some popular Christian music. This lifts my spirits and, more importantly, gives praise to God.

When I was single, I loved to try out different churches. I had my regular one that I went to faithfully, but sometimes it was an adventure to try out something completely different. Most of us are raised in one church and continue in that church building or denomination for the rest of our lives. One Christmas many years ago, an African-American

woman I worked with invited me to her church concert. It was in an unfamiliar part of San Francisco. It was in an unfamiliar church. It was fantastic. My friend I brought along and I were the only white people in the
whole church. It didn't matter. The music and the people transported us.
It was the first time I had ever heard real gospel music. I had tears running down my face, it was so beautiful. I had new enthusiasm and oomph
for my worship life as a result of that experience.

Although these tricks can kick-start a sagging faith walk, they are not
substitutes for the real thing. There are no shortcuts or tricks for developing a mature lifetime relationship with God. One of my favorite
hymns, "Trust and Obey," puts it perfectly. The words are simple and
maybe sometimes a little trite. But I know they are straightforward and
correct. The message in that hymn is similar to my favorite Bible passage
from Proverbs:

> Trust in the Lord with all your heart and lean not on
> your own understanding; in all your ways acknowledge him,
> and he will make your paths straight. Do not be wise in your
> own eyes; fear the Lord and shun evil. This will bring health
> to your body and nourishment to your bones (3:5–8).

Growing Points

1. ✍ Do you have any tricks you do in the garden or with cut flowers?

2. ✍ Have you ever been to another church outside of your denomination for a service other than a wedding or a funeral?

3. ✍ If you could pick a service (Baptist, Catholic, charismatic, Episcopalian, Greek Orthodox, Jewish, Lutheran, Methodist, Pentecostal, modern nondenominational, etc.), which would you pick to experience and why?

4. ✍ What Christian biography or novel has been helpful to you?

Old-Fashioned

In this new millennium, I find it fascinating to see people reach back for the reliable, dependable, simpler things in life. Despite the time-saving benefits of our monthly planners, pagers, faxes, computers, and other digitized paraphernalia, people are turning off and turning in. Inside, that is, to comfort. In my bathroom we have the book *How to Simplify Your Life*. The cooking magazine I receive each month just had an article about casseroles, the supreme comfort food of the 1950s. Along with books and articles about simplicity and comfort food, people are returning to simple, comfortable living.

Faith Popcorn, trend guru, calls this movement *cocooning*. This makes sense to me. After all the whizzing, banging, and clanging of traffic, computers, and cell phones, we are on sensory and information overload with our so-called conveniences. We want a place of solace where we can find comfort food, comfortable furniture, and old-fashioned values. We want the security and solace we feel at Grandma's house. Now even Grandma's garden is back in vogue.

Gone are the temperamental exotic plants that need lots of fussing; in are the old standbys. Flowers evoking memories of simpler times and visits to Grandma's house are replacing yesterday's garish hybrids. Hollyhocks waving hello over white picket fences, sunflowers nodding to sleep in the late afternoon sun, and morning glories' faithful greeting now fill the gardener's bed who has embraced these old-fashioned performers.

As Martha Stewart would say, this is a good thing. There's a reason these flowers have survived so many years despite changing fads and tastes: They are reliable. Old-fashioned flowers can be counted on; they don't need any special care. Year after year they come back. They guarantee a successful and charming garden.

I don't know why such reliable performers ever went out of style. What's not to like about flowers that show up faithfully, year after year, put on a good show, are great for cutting, and don't succumb to disease or pests? Today's gardeners are rediscovering what our grandmothers knew all along: Sunflowers, hollyhocks, daisies, morning glories, black-eyed Susans, coneflowers, bachelor's buttons, cosmos, and cleome (just to name a few) are outstanding heirlooms that will never let your garden down.

Not content just with old-fashioned flowers, some gardeners desire flowers with a pedigree, with historical significance. Thomas Jefferson's Monticello gardens are a great starting place. Our third president and drafter of the Declaration of Independence was a passionate gardener. And because Jefferson was such a passionate collector of plants, you can have a piece of his garden in your own garden.

The Monticello Garden Shop[1] sells plants propagated from the very plants Jefferson collected during his sixty years of gardening, such as twinleaf (*Jeffersonia diphylla*). The online catalog describes twinleaf as follows:

> This rare and desirable native woodland perennial was named to honor Thomas Jefferson in 1792 by the "Father of American Botany," Benjamin Smith Barton. The plant was grown by Jefferson at Monticello, in one of the oval beds planted in 1807.... Twinleaf is well worth growing for its lush green leaves, which make a beautiful groundcover for a shaded site.... Small white flowers resembling those of Bloodroot (*Sanguinaria canadensis*) appear on stems in early spring, before the leaves have expanded.... Prefers shade and woodsy, moderately moist soils. Reaches ten inches high and twelve inches wide. Herbaceous Perennial.

If you would rather have a piece of Jefferson's mind than one of his plants, copies of his garden journal are for sale. The journal chronicles his years of cultivating the flower and vegetable gardens, vineyards,

---

[1] See *www.monticello.org/shop*.

and orchards of Monticello. It is filled with his notations, letters, and thoughts about gardening. In addition to his garden journal, copies of his original farm journal are also available. It is the most complete record of plantation activity in early America.

Reaching back to old-fashioned ideals is happening in churches as well. Churches today are focusing more on the basics, like prayer, but it wasn't always this way. During the 1980s and early '90s, it seemed as if most of the seminars were on church growth. Everybody was talking about numbers, how to bring up the head count, how to offer a zillion differ-ent McPrograms to build the flock into a giant McChurch. Seminars were held on marketing and making our churches more user-friendly. Not that any of those things is bad; but I think we've been dazzled by all the speakers, statistics, and information, while we still have the same old problems. In the midst of a go-go-go economy, people are hurting, going hungry, and dying for some love, while we're cocooning with our catalogs.

The words of the prophet Micah point us back to where our focus should be: "He has showed you, O man, what is good. And what does the Lord require of you? To act justly and to love mercy and to walk humbly with your God" (Micah 6:8). I notice that while I want legal justice to be meted out to others, I desire mercy for myself. I notice that living in Sil-icon Valley, the nation's hot zone for instant billionaires and bravado, humility is not a treasured value.

But I do see it cropping up here and there. In Jim Cymbala's book, *Fresh Wind, Fresh Fire*, he describes how his church, the Brooklyn Tabernacle,

began with a handful of people ("Even I didn't want to show up for a service—that's how bad it was," he wrote) and eventually grew to a church with
a worldwide reputation for prayer and worship. It started with a prayer
meeting of fifteen to eighteen people that expanded to over a hundred
committed prayer warriors.

> We never knew who might come to Christ at the Brook-
> lyn Tabernacle. There were junkies, prostitutes, and homo-
> sexuals. But lost lawyers, business types, and bus drivers
> turned to the Lord there, too. We welcomed them all. There
> were Latinos, African Americans, Caribbean Americans,
> whites—you name it. Once people were energized by the Holy
> Spirit, they began to see other races as God's creation.
> Instead of railing at homosexuals, we began to weep over
> them.... Because I had been a basketball player, it never
> dawned on me to evaluate people on the basis of color. If you
> could play, you could play. In America it would appear that
> there is more openness, acceptance, and teamwork in the
> gym than in the church of Jesus Christ.[2]

James, the brother of Jesus, spoke of values besides church growth
when he described pure religion: "Religion that God our Father accepts
as pure and faultless is this: to look after orphans and widows in their

---

[2] Jim Cymbala, *Fresh Wind, Fresh Fire* (Grand Rapids, Mich.: Zondervan, 1997).

distress and to keep oneself from being polluted by the world" (James 1:27). This old-fashioned outlook toward social justice seems too liberal or foreign for us in this economy of unprecedented financial growth and ubiquitous SUVs. But it wasn't too liberal or foreign for William Booth, Dorothy Day, and Mother Teresa.

William Booth (1829–1912) was the founder of the religious and humanitarian organization, the Salvation Army. He believed religion should alleviate the suffering of the poor and convert sinners. He didn't need a *WWJD* bracelet. In his last speech to the public on May 9, 1912, he said,

> While women weep, as they do now, I'll fight;
> while children go hungry, as they do now, I'll fight;
> while men go to prison, in and out, in and out, as they do
> now, I'll fight;
> while there is a drunkard left, while there is a poor lost girl
> upon the streets, while there remains one dark soul
> without the light of God, I'll fight—
> I'll fight to the very end!

Dorothy Day (1897–1980) started the Catholic Worker movement in New York City. This movement was about justice not being a project for the government, but for you and me, here and now. Her creed was to help feed and clothe the homeless and destitute, offering hospitality and mercy. "We are here to celebrate him through these works of mercy," she said to a friend once. And she was fond of a saying from the early church, "Every home should have a Christ room in it, so that hospitality may be practiced." Hospitality, she explained, was about practicing God's mercy toward those around us. Christ is in the stranger, in the person who has no place to go and no one to welcome him.

And then there's the example of Mother Teresa of Calcutta (1910–1997), whose work with the dying in India's filthy streets is world renowned. This tiny woman, who shunned material possessions, money, and power, found that heads of state and the most powerful people in the world rose to their feet when she entered the room. Such can be the power of old-fashioned values, of loving one another, of serving the poor, and of practicing hospitality for the homeless.

Jesus himself talked about the principles that were the guideposts for the fore-mentioned workers in their service. In Matthew 25:35–40 He states,

> For I was hungry and you gave me something to eat, I was thirsty and you gave me something to drink, I was a stranger and you invited me in, I needed clothes and you clothed me, I was sick and you looked after me, I was in prison and you came to visit me. Then the righteous will answer him, "Lord, when did we see you hungry and feed you, or thirsty and give you something to drink? When did we see you a stranger and invite you in, or needing clothes and clothe you? When did we see you sick or in prison and go to visit you?" The King

will reply, "I tell you the truth, whatever you did for one of the least of these brothers of mine, you did for me."

In the good ol' days, Christians were known for feeding the hungry, leading the drive for the abolition of slavery, and founding educational institutions and hospitals. Today they're known to the secular world for carrying "God hates fags" placards at the funerals of homosexuals.

Despite the tremendous work today of Christian organizations such as World Vision,[3] which feeds, clothes, and educates impoverished children around the world, the press focuses in on the ridiculous things Christians do in God's name. And unfortunately, these people give the press ample material to focus on.

When people clench their fists and declare, "We oughtta git back to old-fashioned values in this country," I wonder if they're referring to our sexual behaviors and voting records or the values that William Booth, Dorothy Day, and Mother Teresa ascribed to. Don't let any political group or government agency hijack this agenda from you; Jesus said these old-fashioned values were His.

---

[3] You can see what World Vision is doing around the world or sponsor a child at *www.worldvision.org* (888-511-6598).

Growing Points

1. ⍟ What are some of your favorite old-fashioned things from your grandparents' time?

2. ⍟ What does "old-fashioned values" mean to you? List some.

3. ⍟ Who do you admire most and why: William Booth, Dorothy Day, or Mother Teresa?

4. ⍟ In Jesus' quotation from Matthew, He lists many opportunities to serve. Which have you done? Which could you do?

It happens all the time. You receive a longed-for invitation from a friend to tour her garden. You've heard other people speak glowingly about it, so you're practically smacking your lips in anticipation. You're so eager to see her tree peonies, her field of naturalized daffodils, or her old-fashioned victory garden.

When the big day arrives, you're in for quite a surprise: her attitude. At first you're dazzled by the display of color, but she shifts your attention when she begins the tour with disparaging comments such as, "Oh, it's too bad you weren't here *last* week. The irises were at their peak! And the tulips, *tsk tsk*. Well, the rabbits got to a lot of them. Of course, the lilacs won't be blooming for another week, so maybe you should come then. It's such a mess, really—sorry. I know I should have deadheaded that plant days ago, but taxes are due...." So instead of focusing on all the glorious foliage and plant combinations, you're treated to a litany of how bad it all looks. I've sung this tune as people have toured my own garden, and I'm sure you've heard it before too.

One midsummer's eve we invited our new neighbors and their two girls over for dinner. The sun was slowly sinking beyond the horizon, painting our predominantly pink-and-white garden in soft, rosy hues as our guests entered our backyard for the patio dinner. The two girls, squealing with delight, did cartwheels around the flower beds. "Ooooh!" they cooed, "this is just like *The Secret Garden!*" I couldn't have been more delighted than if I'd won a landscape design contest. However, I then proceeded to point out all the flaws to their mother as she complimented me on the garden. "I should really have staked those dahlias," I said, pooh-poohing her admiration. "And the cosmos really need to be deadheaded...." I suddenly realized I was pointing out the faults instead of accepting graciously the compliments and focusing on what was *right* with the garden. I was treating my garden as if we were evaluating a finished work of art, like a painting, instead of something constantly in a state of flux.

The garden is, by nature, a living, growing thing. Because some plants are growing and some are finishing their bloom or are declining, the garden is always in a state of change. Therefore, it is never finished. Even if I've spent the whole weekend getting my garden neat and tidy, I know it won't stay that way. Weeds crop up, plants die, pests attack; it's always something. It will never be at that perfect state where I

won't need to work in it again.

For example, it takes a while for some perennials to hit their stride. They're not like the bedding annuals you buy at the nursery, already blooming with all they've got to show.

I went to a specialty nursery once and bought old-fashioned roses on their own roots. The rosebushes seemed puny and pathetic to me, not at all like the robust ones you see in the Jackson and Perkins catalogs (which are grafted roses). But the people at Vintage Gardens[1] assured me that these "own-root" roses would really hit their stride the following year. "Just be patient," they said. They were right. So I didn't mind that they weren't huge, robust rosebushes the first year. I didn't expect them to pump out masses of blooms. They were in transition. It would take a while.

I wish I could be this patient and understanding with my spiritual development. I've had mountaintop moments when I've felt like *I've arrived!* God has shown me an important lesson and I fully *get it!* I'm heady with the clarity of it all. Everything is so much simpler, less complicated. I wonder why it took me so long to understand the lesson. I think that I'll never again struggle so much in my Christian walk. Up there on the mountaintop, everything is so clear; I think I won't have to struggle in this area again.

But life, like the garden, isn't stagnant; things change. So months later, I discover that I'm down in the pit again. I think, *How did this happen?*

---

[1] Vintage Gardens, 707-829-2035 or *www.vintagegardens.com.*

I thought I learned this lesson once and for all. I've longed for the day when I'll have that great and mighty *Aha!* That one glorious insight that I'll never forget, never turn back from, that will propel me to a new standing of Christian maturity and confidence. But our spiritual work is never finished. There will never be that one big moment that solves it all forever, amen. Oh, how I've wished for a maintenance-free Christianity.

According to the second law of thermodynamics, this isn't a possibility. Everything is constantly breaking down; everything needs maintenance—especially our walk with God. Remember those T-shirts that said, "Be patient with me, God's not finished with me yet"? We should apply that thought to ourselves and to others. Someone cut you off on the freeway? Someone jump in front of you in line? Try to remember this: Most people are, just like you, doing the best they can. Instead of muttering to ourselves *How could that person do that?!* we should afford each other grace, realizing that we are all works in progress. God's not finished with us yet; we are always in a state of flux.

I used to believe that the apostles and the prophets in the Bible never had to struggle with this. The first time I read the apostle Paul's letters to the Galatians, Ephesians, and Philippians, I was blown away by the lucidity and power of his intellect. What logic! What encouragement! What a mountaintop view of our great God! I assumed that Paul had arrived. He couldn't possibly have struggled like I do on a daily basis. Fortunately, as mentioned earlier, Paul was honest in his writings. He records, "I do not understand what I do. For what I want to do I do not do, but what I hate I do.... For I have the desire to do what is good, but I cannot carry it out" (Romans 7:15, 18). He struggled like we do.

Even the apostle Peter, who walked with Jesus daily, who ate with Jesus, who saw Him do miracles—even *he* had a major faith setback. Imagine being Jesus' friend and then, at His greatest hour of need, looking Jesus in the eye in front of the authorities who are interrogating Him and saying, "I don't know him." How terrible would we feel? We'd probably think it was because of our testimony that He was killed. We would have no hope that we could ever be forgiven for such a crime. Yet Jesus forgave Peter. Jesus not only forgave him, He healed Peter's shame and commissioned him to go out and "feed" Jesus' followers.

Paul and Peter demonstrate to us that no matter how intimately we know Jesus, we are works in progress. We fail, falter, embarrass ourselves, and let others down. I tend to beat myself up over stuff like that, so I have taped to my computer, "This I know, that God is *for* me" (Psalm 56:9 NASB). I try to be more gentle with myself these days. I try not to focus on my failures and instead focus on my hope, becoming more like Jesus Christ. After all, we are told in Philippians 1:6: "For I am confident of this very thing, that He who began a good work in you will perfect it until the day of Christ Jesus" (NASB).

Growing Points

1. ∽ What are some mountaintop moments you've had in your faith?

2. ∽ What are some areas with which you continually struggle?

3. ∽ What are some areas in which you are making progress?

4. ∽ Read Hebrews 12:2 and Philippians 3:13–14. How do these verses encourage you?

❧

"I can't have a garden like this," she said, sweeping her arm over the view of my garden. "Gardening is hopeless with *my* soil conditions!" Now, I have cement-hard clay soil, plus oak root fungus disease in my soil (which kills things), so I couldn't imagine anyone having soil that *nothing* would grow in.

"What's wrong with your soil?" I asked.

She sighed with resignation, "When we moved in, we got out the Rototiller, started it up, and nearly had our arms jolted out of the sockets. Seems that just below the surface is all shale. Solid rock. It's impossible."

Everyone has obstacles to overcome in gardening. If you're looking for a gardening experience without obstacles, forget about gardening. Even if you've moved to an established garden in England with perfect conditions, you are going to have obstacles. Some gardeners start out with big problems. Steep slopes, high altitude, short growing seasons, heavy wind, diseased soil, swampy soil, sandy soil, arid soil, all rock and no soil, too shady, too sunny, too cold, too hot, too small, ugly views of buildings or telephone poles, or just plain ugly plots. Other gardeners have problems develop along the way. Some years there won't be enough rain, some years there will be too much rain, some plants will become invasive, some plants will become diseased, some pests will arrive—*some*thing is always happening to make it a challenge! If something isn't happening to challenge you, you're not gardening.

When we first moved into our present home, I found the yard depressing. Although some lovely, fragrant jasmine grew in the front yard, oak root fungus lurked in my soil. This meant that half of the jasmine was dead and the other half was threatened. The fungus had killed a large tree in the middle of the lawn, but the previous owners hadn't removed it. They had left it as a welcoming present for us.

Smack in the middle of the backyard, in the sunniest spot, was a big ugly tree. It actually wasn't a tree at all, but an overgrown privet that had been allowed to grow into some semblance of a tree. It dominated the backyard. Underneath, the grass was patchy and weedy. The "lawn" wasn't really a lawn, but a collection of a zillion different weeds that grew close together and looked green and lawnlike. An ugly, decaying old fence bordered all sides of the yard, and it sagged just enough so the neighbors on the left had a full view of our yard and into our windows. The sagging fence on the other side let us

view and hear the elderly couple talking in loud voices over their pool as they cleaned it daily. These neighbors also have metal garbage cans (right near our bathroom and bedroom windows), which they seem to wrestle with every other day. My husband and I are convinced that our neighbor is out there secretly practicing the jitterbug with those metal cans. We have a glassed-in atrium master bath, which is lovely. But because the fence wasn't high enough for total privacy for my six-foot frame, whenever I was taking a shower and heard the metal cans clanking around, I would duck and crouch in the shower until I thought the man was back in his house. I'm sure I looked like someone who had seen the movie *Psycho* one too many times.

Probably the ultimate hurdle I had to face was freeway noise. About two hundred yards across the street is a busy four-lane freeway. Actually, make that *eight* lanes, four each way. You can't see it behind the houses and trees, but you can definitely hear it. Sort of like the constant roar of a stadium crowd. One of my friends tried to be encouraging when she said, "Just pretend it's the roar of the ocean!" Before we replaced our front windows, we had a dinner guest who innocently asked, "Is it raining outside?" I cringed and said, "No, that's the freeway you hear." I hate that noise. I used to fantasize that we would have a severe earthquake that would ruin that stretch of freeway for about a year, so we could have peace and quiet. Or maybe sell our house under the pretense that it's in a quiet neighborhood. I can wail and complain all I want about the noise, but it's not going to change. I had to learn to work around it and, yes, even see the bright side. Everything is close and accessible to us; we're seconds from the freeway!

What I wanted was a lush, lovely secret garden. What I got was a haphazard, noisy mess with little or no privacy.

I could have been like the woman who sighed, "Gardening is hopeless with *my* soil conditions." And, in truth, I felt like that at times. But this was also my first real plot of land to call my own. No more "gardening" in flower pots or apartment windowsills; I finally had my own little piece of dirt and I was happy to put my all into it.

I don't always take this approach with tough situations in my life. I've wasted many months, sometimes years, on inaccessible fantasies—my perfect life script. Like finding Mr. Perfect (as if I were Ms. Perfect). Oh, the time I wasted in that pursuit! I think everyone consciously or unconsciously carries this life script around in his or her heart. It's the play where everything works out great. You marry the perfect person, you have a perfect family life, you have no money or relationship problems, you enjoy praise and compliments from work, you have a great family and friends, you enjoy perfect health, and your garden is, of course, perfect. When things don't work out like our script, we are very unhappy—even bitter—people.

Renee Bondi could have been a bitter person. Her life script didn't work out the way she had planned and hoped. She was in love and engaged. One night she was sleeping peacefully in bed. Suddenly she woke up. She found herself in a bizarre, twisted position, lying halfway out of her bed with her head down near the floor. She became a quadriplegic. She doesn't know how it happened to this day. When I saw her, she had lived with this for several years and was singing in front of our church congregation with a radiant face. Her fiancé had gone ahead with their plans and married her, and she now had a rewarding life teaching others music, singing, and speaking around the country. She was also thrilled to be singing, because at first the doctors didn't think she'd even be able to breathe on her own. It wasn't the plan she had envisioned for her life, but she created something beautiful out of it. She is a living example of the phrase "Bloom where you are planted."

My sister has a friend I'll call Vicky. Her life went in a direction she didn't plan for either. Did you ever see the movie *Lorenzo's Oil*? It's about a little boy with a very rare genetic disease that slowly turns his healthy, happy two-year-old brain to mush. Vicky had to watch two sons slowly die from this horrible disease. You wouldn't know it to look at her today. She is the happy mother of two adopted children. But you can be sure it wasn't easy to get there.

I am humbled and inspired when I consider these women's lives. They took tough situations that others would consider impossible and cultivated productive lives in which love and joy have taken root. It certainly puts our minor inconveniences into a whole new light, doesn't it? It's so easy to think, *I'll be happy and productive when I have more time, our bills are paid, the kids are in school (or out of school), my husband changes, we move, etc.* It's so easy to complain and focus on what we don't have instead of making something beautiful with what we do have. It's so easy to crumple into a chair when confronted with life's difficulties and say, "It's impossible."

Cultivating a meaningful life in the midst of tough situations is never impossible. And we shouldn't be surprised when life *does* confront us with tough situations. That's what life is all about; it's not supposed to be one long tea party. One of my favorite Bible verses is an odd one. Hebrews 5:8 says about Jesus, "Although He was a Son, He learned obedience from the things which He suffered" (NASB). Even Jesus had to *learn* things the hard way. He suffered too. If He suffered, why am I so annoyed and surprised over my minor sufferings here on earth?

If you are part of the human race, you will encounter life's tough situations. If you are going to be a gardener, you will have tough situations too. Our neighbor still bangs his metal garbage cans around, but now I've planted a row of redwood trees as a privacy hedge. The privet "tree" is gone in the backyard; I had it taken out. In its place are rose beds. (The lawn still needs work.) The fences have all been replaced, but the noisy freeway is still there. However, I discovered the beauty and usefulness of fountains. Now we hear our fountain in the backyard instead of the freeway. The oak root fungus is still there, but I've learned which plants will not be killed by it. I've learned to work around the obstacles. To me, that's the challenge and satisfaction of gardening. Now when visitors come into our backyard, they exclaim, "Oh! It's so beautiful and private. I wish my garden was like this." And I tell them, "It can be."

Growing Points

I. ❧ What tough conditions are you facing in life?

2. ❧ What distractions or work-arounds (like redwood trees and fountains) can you use in your tough situation?

3. ❧ What lessons, comfort, or wisdom from your experience could you pass on to others?

4. ❧ Can you think of any blessings or good things that have resulted from your ordeal?

Stewardship

❧

I don't think you really grasp the concept of stewardship until you tend a garden. Before that, it's just a concept, introduced to you by your kids because of their recycling lesson at school. Or maybe you've seen a TV news report about wild-eyed "Greenies" chaining themselves to trees and talking about caring for the earth. From opposing political agendas we hear the occasional sound bite about the depletion of the ozone layer and global warming. But until you become a gardener, you don't really care all that much. About gardeners, Henry Mitchell said, "No class of folk is more keenly aware of how shaky the world is."

I remember an antipollution ad of the 1970s that showed a stream full of trash and chemicals in the background. In the foreground, there was a Native American, Iron Eyes Cody, with a tear running down his cheek. This was so long ago most people think, *Well, that was the seventies, thank God we took care of that.* In history class we saw the Dust Bowl pictures of the 1930s, when the soil was blown away due to poor cultivation practices. The result was a disaster.

Do you know something? Our earth's topsoil is *still* eroding away, and our pollution problems are even worse than in the 1970s. Today, soil on cultivated land in the United States is eroding about sixteen times faster than it can form. Howard-Yana Shapiro and John Harrisson, in their book, *Gardening for the Future of the Earth*, say, "Each year two million acres of arable land in the United States are lost to soil erosion, most of it entirely preventable. Worldwide, about 30 percent of cropland has been lost to soil erosion in the last forty years of the twentieth century."[1] We seem to have forgotten our history lessons. Franklin D. Roosevelt's words haunt us decades later, "The nation that destroys its soil destroys itself."

Nobody wants to hear about history or stewardship these days. Like Bill Clinton's political campaign stated, "It's the economy, stupid." This is all we hear about—or want to pay attention to—in a booming economy. But sometimes, we are brought up close and personal with issues that make it hard to ignore our responsibility, our stewardship, to God's earth.

My husband and I recently bought some rural acreage, forty, to be exact. It's a gorgeous piece of land with a view of the ocean. We hope to build a home and live there someday, but right now there is no power and

---

[1] Howard-Yana Shapiro, Ph.D., and John Harrisson, *Gardening for the Future of the Earth* (New York: Bantam Doubleday, 2000).

no building on the site. (We recently put in a well, and we'll use solar power like everyone else on the mountain does.) We've purchased a small, pop-up camper for when we want to go there and bliss out. Now that I'm face-to-face with the environment, I think twice about which products I buy.

Our camper has a sink with a drain that empties directly underneath the camper. I can watch the sink drain my standard cleanser—or my favorite kind with bleach—out onto the grass. Under the camper live some gophers. Personally, I can't stand gophers; they are a gardener's nightmare. But sometimes at night I've seen skunks wander around and sometimes we see owls. We also share the property with quail, bluebirds, bobcats, coyotes, rabbits, and—our neighbors tell us—foxes and a mountain lion. When I watch the phosphates and other chemicals draining into the soil, I think about these animals. I think about how the water we'll drink will be from our well directly under our property. What's watered into our property will eventually go into our drinking water. I'm starting to think twice about what I allow to drain onto our soil. I'm thinking a lot more about stewardship these days.

This has given me pause at home too. I'm thinking about all the products I use with abandon in the laundry, kitchen, bathrooms, and yard. In the suburbs, the drainage issue is invisible to us. Household wastes, pesticides, and fertilizers from our toilets, sinks, and lawns go down the drains. But where does it go from there? We assume it travels to a water treatment facility and is safely issued out into our waterways, lakes, and oceans. Think again.

Even our seemingly good fertilizers make a negative impact on our environment. According to a report by the National Academy of Sciences,[2] the runoff of excess nutrients from fertilizers is responsible for the death of fish and other marine animals in more than a third of the nation's coastal areas. The fertilizers cause a disproportionate growth of phytoplankton and other organisims (aka algae bloom), which rob fish and other marine life, including plants, of oxygen. This algae bloom is responsible for the decline of fisheries, the death of manatees along the Florida coast, and the death of coral reefs and sea grasses. Although heavy agricultural use is the main culprit, we can do our part by not contributing to the mess. We can stop using "miraculous" chemical fertilizers and learn organic gardening methods.

We should also be concerned about what's leaking into our drinking water. We bathe in it, drink it, cook our food in it, and end up breast-feeding it to our infants. If you think I'm being hysterical, just check the news. Today in our paper there was a story about yet another *E. coli* bacterium contamination of drinking water. The outbreak sickened seven hundred people, and at least five people have died.

Another article in today's paper talks about mounting concern over whether erosion caused by the Los Alamos fire in the summer of 2000

---

[2] Copies of the report are available at *www.national-academies.org*.

will unleash toxic and radiological contaminants into the waterways. Every year in July, the region experiences monsoon-type rains. These could release low-level nuclear and chemical wastes from half a dozen dumps into waterways. Jim Danneskiold, a lab official, says, "There definitely will be movement of contaminated sediments off lab property. It's a question of when, not if, the flood waters come through."

Although Psalm 24:1 says, "The earth is the Lord's, and everything in it, the world, and all who live in it," we don't act as if this is true. A cursory search for the word *stewardship* on the Internet brought up many evangelical Christian sites. But they all talked about money—where to invest it and how to appropriately handle it. God's earth, our environment, was never mentioned (or hard to find).

The Bible talks about our responsibility to be good stewards, to tend God's handiwork. Genesis 2:15 says, "The Lord God took the man and put him in the garden to work it and care for it." Why do we leave this care to the "Greenies"? Why is the fringe element of society the one on the forefront of caring about stewardship of our environment? Author Eugene Linden, in an article for *Time* magazine, asks these questions too. He writes,

> What will it take for us to get serious about saving our environment? When will environmentalism move from being a philosophy promoted by a passionate minority to a way of life that governs

mainstream behavior and policy? How can we understand that Earth is one big natural system and that torching tropical rain forests and destroying coral reefs will eventually threaten the well-being of towns and cities everywhere?3

I think the reasons Christians don't pay attention to stewardship of our environment are a lack of biblical education on stewardship and a lack of passion. We hear confusing and competing sound bites about the environment. Big business and certain groups want us to believe everything is okay. Other political and scientific groups want us to believe our situation is dire. Who's right? Who cares when we are swamped with soccer games, carpools, homework, bills, and demanding work schedules?

The women who started Mothers Against Drunk Driving weren't always passionate about drunks on the road. The problem didn't touch their lives. But then drunk drivers murdered their children. Their lives would never be the same. They now care passionately.

The people who lived on Love Canal, site of a toxic waste dump in the late 1970s, didn't much care about the environment until their health and community became affected. Once they realized they were living on top of 130 pounds of dioxin (just three ounces can kill over a million people), they became passionately concerned. I hope we don't all have to be irrevocably harmed before we decide to do our part. I hope an understanding about how God views the earth He has made and our role in it

---

3 *Time* magazine, Special Edition, Earth Day 2000, Spring 2000, 18.

is enough to motivate us toward good stewardship.

What is stewardship? The Coalition for Christian Colleges and Universities (CCCU) who participated in the 1995–96 Global Stewardship Initiative came up with this definition in their mandate: "Stewardship begins with the understanding that God in Jesus Christ has created and now sustains the world, and that the creation has been entrusted to humans, who were created in God's image...scripture teaches that the chief purpose of creation is to glorify God. As we make use of creation and carry out our stewardly care, we must ensure that creation continues to testify to God's glory. Stewardship care is therefore a trust from God."4

Christians should be the ones leading the charge for good stewardship because God told us to. Some people think that when God said we would rule over the earth (Genesis 1:26, 28), He meant, "Do whatever you want to." God didn't give us license to pour chemicals into the ground, oceans, and sink drains; fill in the Everglades; strip-mine; deforest; throw cigarette butts out the car window; and "rule" with an arrogant, irresponsible attitude. That's not what rule means.

Stewardship is more—it's a delegation of responsibility. If your employer gives you authority over a group of people, if you are a parent, if you lead a scout troop, it doesn't mean you have the right to be—nor do you want to be—the Idi Amin of your little fiefdom. We are not to squander the resources entrusted to us, abuse our authority, lay waste the land given to us to work with, and dump and pollute without compunction. We

---

4 Global Stewardship: The Christian Mandate, *www.cesc.montreat.edu/GSI/ChMand.html*.

are to behave responsibly and with an awareness that our employer, the owner of everything we work with (God himself) is looking over our shoulder and expects good results.

Here's a simple illustration to explain the heart of stewardship. Picture yourself leaving on a trip. You've asked a friend or someone you trust to house-sit while you are gone. They are in charge of your pets and your plants and the overall safety of your home. When you return, what sort of condition would you expect to see your home in? How would you feel if the water supply was polluted, the house was a mess, and some of your plants were dead? You'd probably be outraged.

Harvard entomologist E. O. Wilson talks about the ethics of our behavior in this area. He says, "More and more leaders of science and religion now pose this question: Who are we to destroy or even diminish biodiversity and thus the creation?"

The Bible offers us an education unto the heart of God and His creation. First of all, God's creation is good. Genesis 1:31: "God saw all that he had made and it was very good." Second, the land is God's, not ours to do with as we please. Leviticus 25:23–24 says, "The land must not be sold permanently, because the land is mine and you are but aliens and my tenants." Third, we have been charged with the responsibility and opportunity to be stewards of this earth. Again, Psalm 24:1 says, "The earth is the Lord's and everything in it, the world, and all who live in it." Fourth, God is involved and cares about His creation. Psalm 104:16–18 says, "The trees of the Lord are well watered.... There the birds make their nests.... The high mountains belong to the wild goats."

God speaks in detail about His creation and the animals He has made. If He didn't care so much for the animals, He could have had Noah build an ark just for his family and not for the animals. It certainly would've taken a lot less time. But apparently, God cares tenderly about all He has made.

Romans 8:21 says, "The creation itself will be liberated from its bondage to decay and brought into the glorious freedom of the children of God." Many people look at this passage and think, *The earth will be back to normal, restored, when Jesus comes; it's not my job*. But that is incorrect. It is *not* our job to thoughtlessly trash His place until He returns.

John 1:2–4 says, "[Christ] was with God in the beginning. Through him all things were made; without him nothing was made that has been made. In him was life, and that life was the light of men." Since Jesus was with God in creating the world, He is concerned about its proper care. If we are concerned about doing what Jesus would do, we should care about what He cares about. Renowned theologian Francis Schaeffer wrote, "If I am to be in the right relationship with God, I should treat the things he has made the same way he treats them."

The late Art Meyer wrote, "Those who understand that the Kingdom of God has come with the arrival of Jesus, know that the Creation can begin to be 'redeemed' right now. Romans 8:21–22 speaks to this theme." We should pay attention to the fact that all creation is

included in the hope for redemption. Hosea 2:18 says, "I will make a covenant for them with the beasts of the field and the birds of the air and the creatures that move along the ground." So, on that day creation will be redeemed. We don't know exactly how, but as Christians, we have the opportunity and responsibility to assist in that process.

What can we do? Little things make a big difference. Recycle. Support organic farmers who are enriching and protecting our soil and environment by shopping at organic food stores. Take used plastic bags or cloth bags with handles to the grocery store.[5] Grow a diversity of heirloom vegetables.[6] Stop using chemical pesticides and fertilizers and practice organic gardening. Make or buy compost. Think twice before tossing chemicals down your drains or storm sewers.

We can speak volumes to those around us and set a good example just by making small choices. Plastic diapers are a major contributor to the shortage of landfill capacity in this country. Because of this and their long-term expense, my stepdaughter, Michelle, is using cloth diapers.[7] (Before you groan about this antiquated approach to diapers, you should

---

[5] L.L. Bean (*www.llbean.com* or 800-441-5713) and Land's End (800-356-4444 or *www.landsend.com*) make tote bags that will last you a lifetime.

[6] Seeds of Change (888-762-7333 or *www.seedsofchange.com*) and Seed Savers Exchange (319-382-5990 or *www.seedsavers.org*) are great sources for heirloom organic seeds.

[7] There are many Web sites devoted to cotton diapers. A great site for comparing them all is *www.borntolove.com*. This Web site has articles that address environmental concerns as well.

know that vast improvements have been made in the design, ease, and efficacy of cloth diapers.)

And finally, vote. Vote for people who have a long view of environmental concerns, not those who fatten your wallet (though I admit that's very tempting). What use will a fat wallet be when our world is too polluted to live in? When the toxic chemicals have poisoned the fish in our oceans, who'll want to buy them? Already the rates of asthma and chemical sensitivity are escalating in this country because of living in our chemical-saturated environment. Let's seek to be good stewards with the beautiful world God has entrusted to us. Then we won't feel like hypocrites when we sing majestic hymns such as "How Great Thou Art" and "This Is My Father's World."

How Great Thou Art

O Lord my God, when I in awesome wonder

Consider all the worlds Thy hands have made,

I see the stars, I hear the rolling thunder

Thy power throughout the universe displayed.

Then sings my soul, my Savior God, to Thee;

How great Thou art, how great Thou art!

Then sings my soul, my Savior God, to Thee;

How great Thou art, how great Thou art![8]

---

[8] "How Great Thou Art," text and music by Stuart K. Hine, 1953, renewed 1981 by Manna Music, Inc.

THIS IS MY FATHER'S WORLD

This is my Father's world, And to my listening ears

All nature sings, and round me rings the music of the

    spheres.

This is my Father's world: I rest me in the thought

Of rocks and trees, of skies and seas; His hand the wonders

    wrought.

This is my Father's world, The birds their carols raise,

The morning light, the lily white, Declare their Maker's

    praise.

This is my Father's world: He shines in all that's fair

In the rustling grass I hear Him pass, He speaks to me

    everywhere.9

---

9 "This Is My Father's World," text ty Malthie D. Babcock and music by Franklin L.
Sheppard.

$\mathcal{A}ppendix$

These are the personalized words and Scriptures my neighbor read to her dying brother in the hospital as she led him to the Lord (see the chapter "Self-Sowers").

1. In God's eyes, every single person is equal; we are all sinners (nice people, bad people, the Pope, Mother Teresa, all pastors and priests, me, *YOU*, all of us).

Romans 3:23 says, "For *all* have sinned and fall short of the glory of God." (This is why we all need a Savior.)

2. Fortunately, God loves us in spite of the fact that we can never measure up.

John 3:16–17 says, "For God so loved [you] the world, that He gave His only begotten Son, that whoever believes in Him should not perish, but have eternal life. For God did not send the Son into the world to judge [your name] the world, but that [you] the world should be saved through Him" (NASB).

3. It is a free gift we can never earn or be good enough for.

Romans 6:23 says, "For the wages of sin is death, but the *free gift of God* is eternal life in Christ Jesus our Lord" (NASB).

4. It is a free gift we can have no matter how awful we are.

Romans 5:8 says, "But God demonstrates His own love toward [you] us, in that *while we were yet sinners, Christ died for [you] us*" (NASB).

5. To receive this gift you must be born again.

John 3:5 says, "Jesus answered, 'Truly, truly, I say to you, unless [you] one is born of water and the Spirit, he cannot enter into the kingdom of God'" (NASB).

6. There is no one else we can or should pray to.

First Timothy 2:5 says, "For there is one God and *one mediator* between God and men, the man Christ Jesus."

Acts 4:12 says, "Salvation is found in no one else, for there is no other name under heaven given to men by which we must be saved."

7. God promises to receive us instantly and immediately.

First John 1:9 says, "If [you] we confess our sins, *He is faithful* and righteous to forgive us our sins and to cleanse us from *all* unrighteousness" (NASB).

Romans 8:1 says, "There is therefore now *no condemnation* for those who are in Christ Jesus" (NASB).

8. All it takes is a simple prayer.

Romans 10:9 says, "If you *confess with your mouth Jesus as Lord, and believe in your heart* that God raised Him from the dead, *you shall be saved*" (NASB).

SAMPLE PRAYER: God, I see now that everyone is a sinner, including me. You promised that it doesn't depend on anything I have done in the past, and I can't earn it. Nobody can earn it. You promised to save me if I would "confess with my mouth Jesus as Lord." Well, this is what I am doing now. Please forgive me for everything. I want the undeserved gift of Jesus as Lord of my life. Thank you for forgiving me. Thank you for receiving me. Amen.

9. God will never leave you.

Romans 8:38–39 says, "For I am convinced that neither death, nor life, nor angels, nor principalities, nor things present, nor things to come, nor powers, nor height, nor depth, nor any other created thing, shall be able to separate us from the love of God, which is in Christ Jesus our Lord" (NASB).

Hebrews 13:5 says, *"I will never desert you nor will I ever forsake you"* (NASB).